FOOD FOR ALL
SEASONS

This book is published in 2014 by Octopus
Publishing Group Limited based on materials
licensed to it by Bauer Media Books, Australia
Bauer Media Books are published by
Bauer Media Pty Limited
54 Park St, Sydney; GPO Box 4088,
Sydney, NSW 2001, Australia
phone (+61) 2 9282 8618; fax (+61) 2 9126 3702
www.awwcookbooks.com.au

BAUER MEDIA BOOKS
Publisher Jo Runciman
Editorial & food director Pamela Clark
Director of sales, marketing & rights Brian Cearnes
Creative director Hieu Chi Nguyen
Art director & designer Hannah Blackmore
Food concept director & food editor Sophia Young
Senior editor Stephanie Kistner

Published and Distributed in the United Kingdom
by Octopus Publishing Group
Endeavour House
189 Shaftesbury Avenue
London WC2H 8JY
phone (+44) (0) 207 632 5400; fax (+44) (0) 207 632 5405
info@octopus-publishing.co.uk;
www.octopusbooks.co.uk

Printed in China with 1010 Printing Asia Limited.

International foreign language rights,
Brian Cearnes, Bauer Media Books
bcearnes@bauer-media.com.au

A catalogue record for this book is available
from the British Library.
ISBN: 978-1-909770-16-4 (hardback)

FOOD FOR ALL
SEASONS

CONTENTS

VEGETABLES

Come summer, the good vegetable garden is ripe for the picking. Summertime crops include beans, corn, tomatoes, zucchini and squash, capsicum and lettuce greens. Harvest them at their peak.

FRUIT

Fruit is simply superb in summer: richly coloured, plentiful and sweetly perfumed. Juicy, full-flavoured berries, peaches, nectarines, mangoes, watermelon and cherries truly are this season's taste delights.

WARM SPICED PRAWNS WITH AVOCADO SALSA

¾ cup (180ml) olive oil

2 shallots (50g), sliced thinly

4 cloves garlic, bruised

1 fresh long red chilli, sliced thinly

2 star anise

2 fresh bay leaves

24 uncooked medium king prawns
(shrimp) (1.2kg)

20g (¾ ounce) butter, chopped

2 tablespoons fresh coriander
(cilantro) leaves

AVOCADO SALSA

2 medium avocados (500g),
chopped finely

½ small red onion (50g),
chopped finely

1 medium roma (egg) tomato (75g),
seeded, chopped finely

1 tablespoon lime juice

¼ cup coarsely chopped fresh
coriander (cilantro)

1 Cook oil, shallots, garlic, chilli, star anise and bay leaves in a small saucepan over low heat for 5 minutes or until oil begins to sizzle; cook a further 2 minutes for flavours to infuse. Remove from heat.

2 Shell and devein prawns, keeping tails intact. Thread each prawn onto a skewer starting at the tail end. Place skewers on an oven tray; season, then dot with butter.

3 Make avocado salsa.

4 Preheat grill (broiler).

5 Place prawns under grill for 1 minute or until just cooked through.

6 Remove and discard garlic from warm oil mixture. Place prawn skewers on a large platter; drizzle with warm oil mixutre. Serve prawns with avocado salsa, scattered wtih coriander leaves.

avocado salsa Place ingredients in a medium bowl, season; stir gently to combine.

prep + cook time 40 minutes serves 6 (as part of a feast)

nutritional count per serving 43.2g total fat (9.1g saturated fat); 2025kJ (484 cal); 1.5g carbohydrate; 22.3g protein; 2.4g fibre

serving suggestion Serve with tortilla chips.

THE LEMON JUICE IN THE PESTO WILL DISCOLOUR THE MIXTURE QUICKLY, SO IT'S BEST TO USE THE PESTO AS SOON AS POSSIBLE. IF YOU DO NEED TO MAKE THE PESTO AHEAD OF TIME, SIMPLY OMIT THE JUICE WHEN PREPARING IT IN STEP 3; STORE, COVERED TIGHTLY, IN THE FRIDGE. WHEN YOU'RE READY, STIR THE JUICE INTO THE PESTO AND CONTINUE WITH THE RECIPE FROM STEP 4.

ZESTY LEMON & ROCKET PESTO SPAGHETTI

2 medium lemons (280g)

500g (1 pound) spaghetti

½ cup (75g) roasted unsalted cashews

⅓ cup (50g) roasted pine nuts

1 cup firmly packed fresh basil leaves

50g (1½ ounces) rocket (arugula)

1 teaspoon sea salt flakes

1¼ cups (100g) finely grated parmesan

1¼ cups (310ml) extra virgin olive oil

100g (3 ounces) rocket (arugula), extra

½ cup watercress sprigs

1 Finely grate rind from one lemon. Remove rind from remaining lemon with a zester (or cut rind into thin strips avoiding the white pith). Squeeze juice from lemons; you will need ¼ cup.

2 Cook spaghetti in a large saucepan of boiling salted water for 8 minutes or until almost tender; drain. Return to pan to keep warm.

3 Meanwhile, to make pesto, blend or process nuts, basil, rocket, juice, salt, 1 cup of the parmesan and 1 cup of the oil until almost smooth. Season to taste.

4 Heat remaining oil in a large frying pan, add pesto, pasta and grated rind; toss until heated through.

5 Serve spaghetti topped with extra rocket, remaining parmesan, lemon zest and watercress sprigs.

prep + cook time 25 minutes **serves** 4

nutritional count per serving 98g total fat (18.3g saturated fat); 5772kJ (1379 cal); 93.4g carbohydrate; 29.3g protein; 7.3g fibre

ZA'ATAR CHICKEN WITH HALOUMI & WATERMELON SALAD

4 x 200g (6½-ounce) chicken
   breast fillets

2 tablespoons za'atar

2 tablespoons olive oil

HALOUMI & WATERMELON SALAD

2 tablespoons red wine vinegar

2 tablespoons olive oil

1 clove garlic, crushed

1 teaspoon caster (superfine) sugar

2 x 180g (5½-ounce) pieces
   haloumi cheese, torn

1 teaspoon za'atar

1 tablespoon olive oil, extra

800g (1½ pounds) seedless
   watermelon, chopped coarsely

¼ cup (75g) pitted kalamata olives,
   halved

½ cup loosely packed fresh mint leaves

1 Cut chicken in half horizontally. Place chicken in a medium bowl with za'atar and oil; toss to coat.

2 Cook chicken on a heated chargrill plate (or barbecue or grill), in batches, over medium heat for 2 minutes each side or until cooked through.

3 Meanwhile, make haloumi and watermelon salad.

4 Serve sliced chicken with salad.

haloumi & watermelon salad Combine vinegar, oil, garlic and sugar in a large bowl. Combine haloumi, za'atar and extra oil in a small bowl. Heat a medium frying pan over high heat; cook haloumi mixture 2 minutes or until golden all over. Add haloumi mixture to large bowl with watermelon, olives and mint; toss gently to combine.

prep + cook time 25 minutes **serves** 4

nutritional count per serving 46.9g total fat (15.2g saturated fat); 3155kJ (754 cal); 16.8g carbohydrate; 65.4g protein; 2.9g fibre

tip The salad can be prepared several hours ahead; cook the haloumi and add the dressing just before serving. If you can't get your hands on za'atar, subsitute with dukkah, a spice, seed and nut mixture.

SPELT PASTA WITH BRAISED CAPSICUM, NUTS & CHILLI

¼ cup (60ml) olive oil

1 medium onion (150g), chopped finely

2 cloves garlic, crushed

1 teaspoon fennel seeds

3 medium red capsicums (bell peppers) (600g), diced

3 medium yellow capsicums (bell peppers) (600g), diced

1 fresh long red chilli, seeded, chopped finely

2 tablespoons tomato paste

1¾ cups (430ml) vegetable stock

2 tablespoons red wine vinegar

375g (12 ounces) spelt fettuccine

1 cup fresh basil leaves

2 tablespoons pine nuts, toasted

½ cup (40g) grated parmesan

1 Heat oil in a large saucepan over medium-high heat; cook onion, garlic and fennel seeds, stirring, for 5 minutes. Add capsicum and chilli; cook, covered, stirring occasionally, for 8 minutes. Stir in tomato paste; cook 2 minutes. Add stock; bring to the boil. Reduce heat; simmer, covered, 25 minutes or until capsicum is very tender. Remove from heat; stir in vinegar. Season to taste.

2 Meanwhile, cook pasta in a large saucepan of salted water until almost tender; drain. Return pasta to pan.

3 Add capsicum mixture to pasta with half the basil; toss to combine. Serve pasta topped with pine nuts, parmesan and remaining basil.

prep + cook time 50 minutes **serves** 4

nutritional count per serving 23.5g total fat (4.4g saturated fat); 2714kJ (648 cal); 81.4g carbohydrate; 24.6g protein; 9.5g fibre

tip Spelt is an ancient form of wheat that has a higher level of protein and wider range of nutrients than ordinary wheat. It still contains gluten, making it unsuitable for coeliacs. You can use any form of long pasta instead of the spelt fettuccine.

ZUCCHINI, CARROT & CORN FRITTERS

2 corn cobs (800g)

2 small zucchini (180g)

1 medium carrot (120g),
    grated coarsely

2 eggs, separated

½ cup (90g) rice flour

2 tablespoons water

2 tablespoons rice bran oil

AVOCADO & CORIANDER SALAD

1 large avocado (320g),
    cut into thin wedges

250g (8 ounces) grape tomatoes,
    quartered

2 tablespoons lemon juice

½ cup loosely packed fresh coriander
    (cilantro) sprigs

1 Trim husks and silks from corn. Using a sharp knife, cut kernels from cobs. Cook corn in a small saucepan of boiling water until tender; drain, cool.

2 Coarsely grate zucchini; squeeze out excess moisture. Combine zucchini, corn, carrot, egg yolks, flour and the water in a medium bowl; season.

3 Beat egg whites in a small bowl with an electric mixer until soft peaks form. Fold egg white into vegetable mixture. Shape mixture into 12 fritters.

4 Heat oil in a large non-stick frying pan over medium heat; cook fritters, in three batches, for 2 minutes each side or until browned and cooked through.

5 Meanwhile, make avocado and coriander salad.

6 Serve fritters with salad.

avocado & coriander salad Combine ingredients in a small bowl; season to taste.

prep + cook time 50 minutes **serves** 4

nutritional count per serving 26.4g total fat (5.2g saturated fat); 1921kJ (459 cal); 38g carbohydrate; 11.7g protein; 11.3g fibre

tip These gluten-free vegetable fritters are designed to be eaten for breakfast or brunch, but may be enjoyed as a snack at anytime of the day.

serving suggestion Serve with Greek-style yoghurt, drizzled with a little extra virgin olive oil.

With the longer days and soaring temperatures of summer the beach is the only place to be. Take relief from the heat in the cooling waves, before heading back to the sand for a beachside barbecue.

READY STEAMED BROWN BASMATI RICE IS AVAILABLE IN PACKETS FROM THE RICE SECTION OF SUPERMARKETS. USE FRESH RICOTTA, SOLD IN WHEELS FROM DELIS AND THE DELI SECTION OF SUPERMARKETS FOR THE BEST TASTE AND TEXTURE. IF HEIRLOOM TOMATOES ARE NOT AVAILABLE, USE BABY GRAPE OR CHERRY TRUSS TOMATOES INSTEAD.

TOMATO & GOAT'S CHEESE TART WITH RICE & SEED CRUST

500g (1 pound) packaged ready-steamed brown basmati rice

⅓ cup (50g) sesame seeds

1½ cups (120g) finely grated parmesan

3 eggs

1 teaspoon sea salt flakes

500g (1 pound) fresh ricotta

150g (4½ ounces) soft goat's cheese

¼ cup (60ml) milk

1 tablespoon wholegrain mustard

1 clove garlic, chopped finely

400g (12½ ounces) mixed heirloom tomatoes, halved and sliced

2 tablespoons small fresh basil leaves

1 tablespoon extra virgin olive oil

2 teaspoons balsamic vinegar

1 Preheat oven to 200°C/400°F. Grease a 24cm (9½-inch) springform pan.

2 Process rice, seeds and half the parmesan until rice is finely chopped. Add 1 egg and half the salt; process until mixture forms a coarse dough.

3 Using damp hands, press rice dough over base and up the side of the pan, stopping 5mm (¼ inch) from the top.

4 Bake crust 25 minutes or until golden and dry to the touch.

5 Meanwhile, process ricotta, goat's cheese, milk, mustard and garlic with remaining parmesan, eggs and salt until smooth.

6 Pour cheese mixture into warm rice crust. Reduce oven to 180°C/350°F; bake tart a further 30 minutes or until a skewer inserted into the centre comes out clean. Cool 1 hour.

7 Just before serving, arrange tomatoes and basil on top of tart; drizzle with oil and vinegar. Season with freshly ground black pepper.

prep + cook time 1 hour (+ cooling) **serves** 8

nutritional count per serving 22.5g total fat (10.5g saturated fat); 1549kJ (370 cal); 20.2g carbohydrate; 21.2g protein; 2g fibre

MEXICAN-STYLE
BARBECUED CORN
(RECIPE PAGE 30)

MEXICAN-STYLE BARBECUED CORN

1 tablespoon chipotle chillies in adobo sauce

2 teaspoons lime juice

1½ cups (450g) whole-egg mayonnaise

2 tablespoons pepitas (green pumpkin seed kernels)

½ teaspoon smoked spanish paprika

½ teaspoon ground cumin

6 cobs corn (1.5kg), in husks

½ cup (40g) finely grated parmesan

3 limes (270g), cut into cheeks

1 Process chillies in adobo sauce with juice and mayonnaise until smooth.

2 Stir pepitas in a dry frying pan over low-medium heat for 3 minutes or until lightly browned. Add paprika and cumin, stir a further 15 seconds. Transfer to a small bowl.

3 Cook corn in husks in a large saucepan of boiling salted water for 6 minutes or until almost tender. Drain; cool in husks. Peel back the corn husks; remove and discard the silks. Tie the husks back with kitchen string.

4 Heat a barbecue or chargrill pan over medium heat; cook corn, turning, for 5 minutes or until lightly charred.

5 Place corn on a platter, spoon a little chipotle mayonnaise on cobs; sprinkle with parmesan, then pepita mixture. Serve with lime cheeks and remaining chipotle mayonnaise.

prep + cook time 35 minutes **serves** 6

nutritional count per serving 67.3g total fat (11.6g saturated fat); 3269kJ (781 cal); 27.7g carbohydrate; 11.8g protein; 11.7g fibre

(photograph page 29)

BREAD & BUTTER PICKLES

500g (1 pound) lebanese cucumbers, unpeeled, sliced thinly lengthways

6 shallots (150g), sliced thinly

¼ cup (70g) coarse cooking salt (kosher salt)

1 cup (250ml) white vinegar

1 cup (220g) white (granulated) sugar

2 teaspoons mustard seeds

½ teaspoon dried chilli flakes

¼ teaspoon ground turmeric

1 Combine cucumber, shallots and salt in a medium stainless steel or glass bowl. Cover; stand 3 hours.

2 Drain, then rinse cucumber mixture; drain on paper towel. Spoon into hot sterilised jars (see tips).

3 Place vinegar and remaining ingredients in a medium saucepan; stir over high heat, without boiling, until sugar dissolves. Bring to the boil; remove from heat.

4 Pour enough hot vinegar mixture into jars to cover cucumber mixture; seal immediately. Label and date jars when cold.

prep + cook time 30 minutes (+ standing) **makes** 4 cups

nutritional count per tablespoon 0g total fat (0g saturated fat); 88kJ (21 cal); 5g carbohydrate; 0.1g protein; 0.2g fibre

tips For information on sterilising jars, see page 236. Bottled pickles will keep for up to 2 months in a cool, dark place. Refrigerate after opening. You can use a single variety of cucumber or a combination of cucumbers such as apple, baby and lebanese cucumbers.

serving suggestions Serve with bread, cold cuts, cheese and salad.

BREAD & BUTTER PICKLES

BANG BANG CHICKEN SALAD

....

1.6kg (3¼-pound) whole chicken

4 green onions (scallions)

2 fresh coriander (cilantro) roots, washed

30g (1 ounce) fresh ginger, sliced thinly

12 black peppercorns

1 tablespoon sea salt

1 litre (4 cups) cold tap water

150g (4½ ounces) green mung bean (cellophane) noodles

1½ tablespoons sesame oil

¼ cup (70g) tahini

2 tablespoons dark soy sauce

2 tablespoons hoisin sauce

2 tablespoons honey

1 teaspoon chilli oil

¼ cup (60ml) warm water

½ cup small fresh coriander (cilantro) sprigs

2 lebanese cucumbers (260g), cut lengthways into long thin strips

3 green onions (scallions), extra, cut lengthways into long thin strips

2 tablespoons sesame seeds, toasted

1 Rinse chicken inside and out. Place green onion, coriander roots, ginger, peppercorns, salt and the tap water in a large saucepan or stock pot; bring to the boil. Carefully add chicken, and more tap water, if necessary, so it is submerged; return to the boil. Cover pan with a tight-fitting lid, turn off the heat; stand chicken in poaching liquid for 2 hours (the remaining heat will finish the cooking process).

2 Remove chicken from pan; strain poaching liquid and reserve for another use. (Strained poaching liquid can be frozen for up to 1 month.)

3 Using your hands, pull legs and breast meat from chicken. Place on a work surface and gently pound each piece with a meat mallet or rolling pin several times to flatten slightly. Remove skin and discard; shred meat using two forks or your fingers, then transfer to a large bowl.

4 Place noodles in a heatproof bowl, cover with boiling water; stand 10 minutes. Drain well. Return noodles to bowl with 1 teaspoon of the sesame oil.

5 Stir tahini, sauces, honey, chilli oil, the warm water and remaining sesame oil in a small bowl until smooth.

6 Arrange noodles in a large serving bowl with shredded chicken, coriander, cucumber and extra green onion; scatter with sesame seeds. Serve drizzled with tahini sauce.

prep + cook time 1 hour (+ standing) **serves** 4

nutritional count per serving 33g total fat (6.3g saturated fat); 2878kJ (688 cal); 22.2g carbohydrate; 73.5g protein; 4.3g fibre

tip Traditionally the sauce for bang bang chicken is made with a Chinese sesame seed paste, this can be tricky to find. However, while not traditional, tahini (sesame seed paste) makes a good substitute.

TOMATO SALAD WITH LABNE & SEEDS

You will need to start this recipe the day before.

2 teaspoons sesame seeds

2 teaspoons sunflower seeds

2 tablespoons coarsely chopped pistachios

2 teaspoons ground cumin

1 teaspoon sea salt flakes

1kg (2 pounds) large and small heirloom tomatoes

½ cup (60g) sicilian green olives

½ small red onion (50g), sliced thinly

3 cups (350g) firmly packed watercress sprigs

¼ cup loosely packed fresh coriander (cilantro) sprigs

LABNE

1 teaspoon sea salt flakes

500g (1 pound) Greek-style yoghurt

DRESSING

¼ cup (60ml) extra virgin olive oil

1½ tablespoons lemon juice

1 clove garlic, quartered

1 Make labne, then dressing.

2 Stir seeds, nuts, cumin and salt in a dry medium frying pan over low heat for 5 minutes or until fragrant. Remove from pan; cool.

3 Halve or thickly slice some of the larger tomatoes; place all tomatoes in a large bowl. Slice cheeks from olives close to the pits; discard pits. Add olives to bowl with onion, watercress, coriander and half the dressing; toss gently to combine. Season to taste.

4 Serve tomato salad topped with labne and seed mixture; drizzle with remaining dressing.

labne Stir salt into yoghurt in a small bowl. Line a sieve with two layers of muslin (or a clean, unused open weave cloth); place sieve over a deep bowl or jug. Spoon yoghurt mixture into sieve, gather cloth and tie into a ball with kitchen string. Refrigerate 24 hours or until thick, gently squeezing occasionally to encourage the liquid to drain. Discard liquid. Roll or shape tablespoons of labne into balls.

dressing Place ingredients in a screw-top jar, season to taste; shake well. Stand at least 20 minutes or refrigerate overnight. Discard garlic before using.

prep + cook time 35 minutes (+ refrigeration) **serves** 4

nutritional count per serving 28.5g total fat (7.8g saturated fat); 1863kJ (445 cal); 29.2g carbohydrate; 13.5g protein; 7.6g fibre

tips Labne can be made 5 days ahead. Refrigerate, covered with olive oil, in a small shallow container. Drain before using. You can use 150g (4½ ounces) crumbled fetta or soft goat's cheese instead of labne. You will need 1 large bunch of watercress for this recipe.

serving suggestion Serve with wholemeal turkish or afghan bread.

BALSAMIC HONEY PULLED-PORK BUNS

800g (1½-pound) piece trimmed
  pork shoulder

2 tablespoons olive oil

1 large brown onion (200g), chopped

4 cloves garlic, peeled

4 sprigs fresh thyme

2 sprigs fresh rosemary

2 cups (500ml) chicken stock

1 cup (250ml) water

4 brioche buns (280g), split

4 trimmed radishes (60g), sliced thinly

COLESLAW

200g (6½ ounces) cabbage,
  sliced thinly

2 tablespoons finely chopped
  fresh chives

¾ cup (150g) mayonnaise

2 tablespoons white wine vinegar

BALSAMIC HONEY BARBECUE SAUCE

3 teaspoons olive oil

1 small brown onion (80g),
  chopped finely

2 cloves garlic, crushed

1 cup (250ml) balsamic vinegar

½ cup (140g) tomato sauce (ketchup)

¼ cup (55g) firmly packed brown sugar

2 tablespoons honey

1 tablespoon worcestershire sauce

1 tablespoon dijon mustard

1 Preheat oven to 160°C/325°F.

2 Season pork. Heat oil in a large heavy-based saucepan over high heat; cook pork for 2 minutes each side or until browned. Add onion, garlic and herbs; cook, stirring, for 2 minutes or until softened. Add stock and the water; bring to the boil. Cover; cook in oven 2 hours. Remove the lid; cook a further 1 hour or until pork is tender.

3 Meanwhile, make coleslaw.

4 Remove pork from pan, cover with foil; set aside. Strain pan juices into a bowl; reserve 1 cup of the juices.

5 Make balsamic honey barbecue sauce.

6 Shred pork using two forks; stir into barbecue sauce. Sandwich buns with coleslaw, pork and radish.

coleslaw Combine ingredients in a large bowl; season to taste. Refrigerate until ready to serve.

balsamic honey barbecue sauce Heat oil in a large saucepan over medium heat; cook onion and garlic, stirring, until softened. Add remaining ingredients and reserved pan juices from pork; bring to the boil. Reduce heat to low; simmer, uncovered, 15 minutes, stirring occasionally, or until mixture has reduced by half. Season to taste.

prep + cook time 3 hours 45 minutes **makes** 4

nutritional count per bun 30.9g total fat (5.1g saturated fat); 4130kJ (987 cal); 114.8g carbohydrate; 56.8g protein; 7.3g fibre

tip You could use pork scotch fillet (neck) for this recipe.

ZUCCHINI FLOWERS WILT AND SPOIL WITHIN A DAY OR TWO. WHEN BUYING, LOOK FOR LARGE, BRIGHT FRESH ORANGE FLOWERS WITH THE GREEN ZUCCHINI ATTACHED. STORE THEM FLAT ON A TRAY, COVERED WITH DAMP PAPER TOWEL THEN WRAP IN PLASTIC WRAP. BE SURE TO PUT THEM WHERE THEY WON'T BE CRUSHED BY OTHER PRODUCE.

LEMON & RICOTTA-FILLED ZUCCHINI FLOWERS

250g (8 ounces) firm ricotta

2 tablespoons finely grated parmesan

1 teaspoon finely grated lemon rind

1 tablespoon lemon juice

1 tablespoon finely chopped fresh mint

2 tablespoons toasted pine nuts

12 zucchini flowers with zucchini
    attached (240g)

vegetable oil, for deep-frying

1 medium lemon (140g),
    cut into wedges

TEMPURA BATTER

¾ cup (105g) plain (all-purpose) flour

½ cup (90g) rice flour

½ teaspoon baking powder

1 egg

1¼ cups (310ml) chilled soda water

1 Combine ricotta, parmesan, rind, juice, mint and pine nuts in a small bowl.

2 Carefully open zucchini flowers, taking care not to tear the petals; remove and discard the yellow stamen inside. Fill with ricotta mixture, twisting the tips of the petals to enclose filling.

3 Make tempura batter.

4 Heat a large saucepan or wok one-third full with oil. In batches, dip flowers in the batter, allowing excess batter to drain off. Deep-fry flowers, in batches, until browned lightly and crisp. Drain on paper towel.

5 Serve immediately with lemon wedges and seasoned with salt.

tempura batter Reserve 1 tablespoon plain flour. Sift remaining plain flour with rice flour and baking powder into a large bowl; stir in egg and soda water until just combined. The batter will still have lumps. Add reserved flour only if the batter seems too thin.

prep + cook time 45 minutes **serves** 4

nutritional count per serving 22.6g total fat (6.1g saturated fat); 1436kJ (343 cal); 23.5g carbohydrate; 11.1g protein; 1.8g fibre

tip Place a small piece of potato in the cold oil and heat with the oil, once the potato is a light golden colour you will know that the oil is sufficently hot to start frying. Discard the potato.

FATTOUSH

180g (5½ ounces) persian fetta in oil

2 tablespoons pomegranate molasses

2 tablespoons lemon juice

1 baby cos (romaine) lettuce (180g),
    leaves separated, torn

1 lebanese cucumber (130g),
    sliced thinly

6 red radishes (300g), sliced thinly

3 green onions (scallions), sliced
    lengthways into thin strips

1 medium green capsicum
    (bell pepper) (200g),
    cut into 2cm (¾-inch) pieces

250g (8 ounces) cherry tomatoes,
    halved

½ cup lightly packed fresh mint leaves

1½ cups (45g) pitta crisps

½ teaspoon sumac

1 Drain oil from fetta into a jug or small bowl; you will need ¼ cup.

2 Whisk pomegranate molasses, reserved fetta oil and juice in a large bowl.
Season to taste. Add lettuce, cucumber, radish, green onion, capsicum, tomatoes
and mint; toss gently to combine.

3 Serve salad topped with crumbled fetta and pitta crisps; sprinkle with sumac.

prep time 20 minutes **serves** 4

nutritional count per serving 20.7g total fat (8.1g saturated fat); 1274kJ (304 cal);
17.7g carbohydrate; 9.1g protein; 4.8g fibre

tips Pitta crisps are available from some delicatessens, greengrocers and specialist
food stores. The dressing can be made a day ahead; refrigerate in a screw-top jar.
Assemble the salad just before serving.

serving suggestion Serve with prawns or sliced barbecued lamb backstraps.

FRIED ASIAN SHALLOTS ARE SOLD IN CELLOPHANE BAGS OR JARS
AT MOST MAJOR SUPERMARKETS AND ASIAN GROCERY STORES;
ONCE OPENED, THEY WILL KEEP FOR MONTHS IF STORED TIGHTLY SEALED.

LETTUCE WEDGES WITH CREAMY LEMON DRESSING

300g (9½ ounces) sour cream

1 cup (300g) whole-egg mayonnaise

1 teaspoon finely grated lemon rind

1½ tablespoons lemon juice

½ medium brown onion (80g)

4 baby cos (romaine) lettuce (720g)

¼ cup (20g) fried asian shallots

¼ cup loosely packed fresh
   flat-leaf parsley leaves

1 Place sour cream, mayonnaise, rind and juice in a medium bowl. Coarsely grate onion into a small bowl. Press down on onion to extract as much juice as possible; discard onion, reserve onion juice. Add onion juice to sour cream mixture, stir to combine; season.

2 Remove outer leaves from lettuce; discard root end. Cut each lettuce into quarters lengthways (if necessary, push a 20cm (8-inch) bamboo skewer through the leaves to hold them together).

3 Arrange lettuce wedges on a large platter. Drizzle with dressing; scatter with shallots and parsley.

prep time 20 minutes serves 8

nutritional count per serving 44.8g total fat (14.1g saturated fat); 1794kJ (429 cal); 4.1g carbohydrate; 2.8g protein; 1.9g fibre

TO HELP REMOVE THE POPSICLE FROM ITS MOULD, USE A DAMP WARM CLOTH AND RUB THE OUTSIDE OF THE MOULDS UNTIL THE POPSICLE IS RELEASED.

RASPBERRY, LIME & LYCHEE POPSICLES

1 cup (220g) caster (superfine) sugar

1 cup (250ml) water

½ cup (125ml) liquid glucose

530g (1 pound) raspberries

⅓ cup (80ml) lime juice

1kg (2 pounds) lychees, peeled

¼ cup (60ml) water, extra

8 wooden paddle pop sticks

1 To make sugar syrup, place sugar, the water and glucose in a small saucepan; cook, stirring, over high heat until sugar dissolves and mixture boils. Remove from heat. Cool.

2 Process raspberries, 2 tablespoons of the juice and ¾ cup of the sugar syrup until smooth. Strain mixture through a fine sieve over a bowl, pushing down on mixture with a wooden spoon to extract all liquid. Discard seeds. Spoon strained mixture into a container; chill in the freezer.

3 Meanwhile, remove seeds from lychees. Process lychee flesh, remaining juice and ½ cup of the sugar syrup and the extra water until smooth. Strain mixture through a fine sieve over a bowl.

4 Spoon or pour 1½ tablespoons lychee mixture into each of eight ⅓ cup (80ml) popsicle moulds; freeze 2 hours or until mostly frozen. Spoon raspberry mixture layer on top.

5 Cover each mould tightly with two layers of plastic wrap. Pierce the wrap with the tip of a knife, then insert a paddle pop stick (the plastic wrap will keep the stick in position). Freeze popsicles 4 hours or overnight until firm.

prep + cook time 30 minutes (+ freezing) **makes** 8

nutritional count per popsicle 0.3g total fat (0.1g saturated fat); 1001kJ (239 cal); 64.2g carbohydrate; 1.9g protein; 5.2g fibre

tips You can use any remaining sugar syrup to make cocktails. Instead of popsicle moulds, you can use interesting shaped diarole moulds or individual jelly moulds, as we have done here. In shallow moulds, use shorter wooden paddle pop sticks.

PEACH FRANGIPANE TART
(RECIPE PAGE 50)

PEACH FRANGIPANE TART

1½ cups (225g) plain (all-purpose) flour

½ cup (80g) icing (confectioners') sugar

125g (4 ounces) cold butter, chopped

1 egg yolk

1 tablespoon iced water, approximately

4 medium ripe peaches (600g)

FRANGIPANE

200g (6 ounces) butter, softened

1½ cups (180g) ground almonds

1 cup (220g) caster (superfine) sugar

½ cup (75g) plain (all-purpose) flour

4 eggs

1 To make pastry, process flour, sugar and butter until mixture resembles breadcrumbs. Add egg yolk and the water; process until mixture just comes together. Shape into a disc; wrap in plastic wrap. Refrigerate 30 minutes.

2 Make frangipane.

3 Grease a 20cm x 30cm (8-inch x 12-inch) slice pan; line base and sides with baking paper. Roll pastry between sheets of baking paper until large enough to line pan. Ease pastry into pan, press into sides; trim edge. Refrigerate 20 minutes.

4 Preheat oven to 180°C/350°F. Line pastry with baking paper; fill with dried beans or rice. Bake 15 minutes. Remove paper and beans; bake 10 minutes or until pastry is golden and dry. Cool.

5 Spread frangipane over base.

6 Halve peaches; remove stones. Cut each half into three wedges. Arrange wedges on top of frangipane.

7 Bake tart 55 minutes or until browned and set (cover with foil if overbrowning). Stand tart 15 minutes before serving.

frangipane Process butter, nuts, sugar and flour until it forms a paste. Add eggs; process until combined.

prep + cook time 1 hour 15 minutes (+ refrigeration & cooling)
serves 12
nutritional count per serving 20.9g total fat (10.6g saturated fat); 1500kJ (358 cal); 36.7g carbohydrate; 5.9g protein; 2.5g fibre
serving suggestion Serve drizzled with cream and honey.

(photograph page 49)

CHOCOLATE, HONEY & RED BERRY PARFAIT

You will need to start this recipe a day ahead.

½ cup (80g) natural almonds

1 vanilla bean

400g (12½ ounces) ricotta

⅔ cup (230g) honey

2 cups (560g) Greek-style yoghurt

100g (3 ounces) dark chocolate (70% cocoa), chopped

100g (3 ounces) raspberries

100g (3 ounces) cherries, halved, pitted

2 tablespoons honey, extra

1 Preheat oven to 180°C/350°F. Grease base of a 9cm (3¾-inch) deep, 23cm (9¼-inch) brioche tin; line base with baking paper (see tip below).

2 Spread nuts in a single layer on an oven tray. Roast 10 minutes or until skins begin to split. Cool. Chop coarsely.

3 Meanwhile, split vanilla bean lengthways; scrape seeds into a food processor. Add ricotta and honey; process until smooth. Transfer mixture to a large bowl.

4 Fold in chopped nuts, yoghurt, chocolate, raspberries and cherries. Spoon mixture into pan; smooth surface. Cover with foil. Freeze 8 hours or overnight until firm.

5 Wipe the base and side of tin with a warm cloth. Turn parfait out onto a platter. Stand 10 minutes before serving, drizzled with extra honey.

prep + cook time 40 minutes (+ cooling, freezing & standing)
serves 8
nutritional count per serving 19g total fat (8.8g saturated fat); 1743kJ (416 cal); 50g carbohydrate; 12g protein; 2g fibre
tip The parfait can also be made in a 10.5cm x 23.5cm (4-inch x 9½-inch) terrine or loaf pan; grease, then line the base and sides with baking paper, extending the paper over two long sides.
serving suggestion Serve with extra raspberries and cherries.

MANGO & COCONUT TRES LECHE CAKE

....

125g (4 ounces) strawberries, chopped

60g (2 ounces) blueberries

60g (2 ounces) raspberries

4 eggs, separated

1 cup (220g) caster (superfine) sugar

⅓ cup (80ml) milk

1 teaspoon vanilla extract

1⅓ cups (200g) plain (all-purpose) flour

1 teaspoon baking powder

395g (12½ ounces) canned sweetened condensed milk

½ cup (125ml) evaporated milk

½ cup (125ml) coconut cream

2 large mangoes (1.2kg), sliced thinly

1 lime (90g), rind grated finely

WHIPPED COCONUT CREAM

¼ cup (60ml) coconut cream, chilled

300ml thickened (heavy) cream, chilled

2 tablespoons icing (confectioners') sugar

½ teaspoon vanilla extract

1 Preheat oven to 160°C/325°F. Grease a 22cm (9-inch) square cake pan; line base and sides with baking paper, extending the paper 5cm (2 inches) over the sides.

2 Combine strawberries, blueberries and raspberries in a small bowl.

3 Beat egg whites in a medium bowl with an electric mixer until soft peaks form. Gradually add sugar, beating until glossy and stiff. Combine egg yolks, milk and extract in a small bowl. With the motor operating, gradually add milk mixture to egg white mixture until well combined. Sift flour and baking powder onto mixture, then gently fold through; fold in berries. Pour mixture into pan; level surface.

4 Bake cake for 1 hour, turning pan halfway through cooking, or until a skewer inserted into the centre comes out clean.

5 Meanwhile, whisk condensed milk, evaporated milk and coconut cream together in a large jug until combined.

6 As soon as the cake is cooked, use a skewer to poke holes in the cake; pour milk mixture over hot cake. Cool cake in pan.

7 Meanwhile, make whipped coconut cream.

8 Spread whipped coconut cream on cake; decorate with mango slices and rind.

whipped coconut cream Push coconut cream through a fine sieve into a small bowl. Beat thickened cream, sifted icing sugar and extract in a small bowl with an electric mixer until almost soft peaks form. Fold in sieved coconut cream.

prep + cook time 1 hour 20 minutes (+ cooling) **serves** 9

nutritional count per serving 10.9g total fat (6.9g saturated fat); 2024kJ (483 cal); 84.5g carbohydrate; 12.2g protein; 3.7g fibre

tips Shake the can of coconut cream before you open it. You can use whatever berries you like, such as mulberries and loganberries. If you have a zesting tool, you can use it to make long thin strips of lime rind instead of grating it. The cake is easier to cut using a flat-bladed knife, rather than a serrated knife. This cake is best made on the day of serving.

NECTARINE & GINGER SOUR CREAM CAKES

. . . .

125g (4 ounces) butter, softened

1 cup (220g) firmly packed
   brown sugar

3 eggs

⅓ cup (80g) sour cream

1 cup (150g) plain (all-purpose) flour

¼ cup (35g) self-raising flour

2 teaspoons ground ginger

¼ teaspoon ground clove

1 tablespoon demerara sugar

POACHED NECTARINES

6 yellow-fleshed nectarines (1kg)

1 cup (220g) caster (superfine) sugar

2 cups (500ml) dry white wine

2 cups (500ml) water

1 cinnamon stick

2 star anise

1 Make poached nectarines

2 Preheat oven to 170°C/340°F. Line a 12-hole (⅓-cup/80ml) muffin pan with paper cases.

3 Beat butter and brown sugar in a medium bowl with an electric mixer until light and fluffy. Beat in eggs, one at a time, until combined. Stir in sour cream and sifted flours and spices. Spoon mixture into paper cases.

4 Working quickly, place nectarine halves, cut-side down, on cake mixture. Using your fingers, push nectarines down slightly into the batter. Sprinkle with demerara sugar.

5 Bake cakes 30 minutes or until a skewer inserted into the centre comes out clean. Stand cakes in pan 5 minutes before transferring to a wire rack to cool.

poached nectarines Slice nectarine cheeks from each side of the stone; discard stone and remaining attached flesh. Stir sugar, wine, the water, cinnamon and star anise in a medium saucepan over high heat, without boiling, until sugar dissolves; bring to the boil. Add nectarines; cover with a small plate to keep nectarines submerged. Reduce heat; simmer for 5 minutes or until nectarines are just tender. Remove nectarines from syrup; when cool enough to handle, peel away skins. Cool completely.

prep + cook time 45 minutes **makes** 12

nutritional count per cake 10g total fat (4.1g saturated fat); 1117kJ (267 cal); 39.1g carbohydrate; 4.3g protein; 2.1g fibre

tip If you like, nectarine poaching liquid can be boiled for 20 minutes or until reduced by half and served as a syrup with the cakes. It can also be used as the base for a fruit salad with stone fruit or berries.

serving suggestion Serve warm with a dollop of double (thick) cream.

YOU CAN ALSO USE PEACHES, APRICOTS OR PLUMS INSTEAD OF NECTARINES. KEEP ANY LEFTOVER POACHING LIQUID TO POACH OTHER FRUIT; OR, SIMMER THE LIQUID UNTIL IT'S REDUCED AND SYRUPY, STIR IN 1 TABLESPOON ORANGE-FLAVOURED LIQUEUR THEN POUR OVER ICE-CREAM.

WHITE CHOCOLATE CREAM WITH POACHED NECTARINES

125g (8 ounces) white chocolate, chopped coarsely

300ml pouring cream

2 tablespoons caster (superfine) sugar

1 vanilla bean, split lengthways

1½ teaspoons powdered gelatine

1 tablespoon boiling water

½ cup (140g) Greek-style yoghurt

¼ cup (20g) flaked almonds, roasted

POACHED NECTARINES

3 medium yellow nectarines (300g)

1 cup (220g) caster (superfine) sugar

2 cups (500ml) water

1 cinnamon stick

1 Stir chocolate, cream, sugar and vanilla bean in a small saucepan over low heat until smooth. Cool 5 minutes.

2 Sprinkle gelatine over the boiling water in a small heatproof bowl. Stand bowl in a small saucepan of simmering water; stir until gelatine dissolves. Stir gelatine mixture into cream mixture. Cool 15 minutes. Discard vanilla bean.

3 Whisk yoghurt into cream mixture until combined. Pour mixture into six 1½-cup (375ml) glasses. Cover loosely with plastic wrap; refrigerate 4 hours or overnight until set.

4 Make poached nectarines.

5 Serve chocolate cream topped with nectarine halves, reserved syrup and nuts.

poached nectarines Halve nectarines; discard stones. Stir sugar, the water and cinnamon in a small saucepan over medium heat, without boiling, until sugar dissolves. Bring to the boil. Reduce heat, add nectarines; simmer, uncovered, 5 minutes or until nectarines are just tender. Cool nectarines in syrup. Discard cinnamon stick. Remove nectarines; discard skins. Reserve ½ cup syrup (keep remaining liquid for another use).

prep + cook time 35 minutes (+ cooling & refrigeration) **serves** 6

nutritional count per serving 28.1g total fat (16.9g saturated fat); 1701kJ (406 cal); 33.8g carbohydrate; 5.7g protein; 1.2g fibre

STRAWBERRY TIRAMISU

½ cup (125ml) pouring cream

½ cup (125g) mascarpone

⅓ cup (75g) caster (superfine) sugar

3 egg yolks

6 sponge finger biscuits (150g)

125g (4 ounces) small strawberries, hulled

STRAWBERRY SAUCE

200g (6½ ounces) strawberries, chopped coarsely

1 tablespoon lemon juice

1 tablespoon icing (confectioners') sugar

1 tablespoon water, approximately

1 Make strawberry sauce.

2 Beat cream, mascarpone and 1 tablespoon of the sugar in a small bowl with an electric mixer until almost firm peaks form. Beat egg yolks and remaining sugar in another small bowl with an electric mixer until thick and creamy. Fold egg yolk mixture into mascarpone mixture.

3 Cut biscuits in half. Pour ¾ cup of strawberry sauce into a small bowl; dip biscuits into sauce. Place soaked biscuits into the base of a 1 litre (4-cup) glass serving bowl. Top with mascarpone mixture, cover; refrigerate 1 hour. Refrigerate remaining strawberry sauce.

4 Just before serving, pour remaining strawberry sauce over mascarpone layer. Serve topped with small strawberries.

strawberry sauce Blend or process strawberries until smooth. Strain puree into a small jug; discard seeds. Stir juice, sugar and enough of the water into puree to make 1 cup of sauce.

prep + cook time 40 minutes (+ refrigeration) **serves** 6

nutritional count per serving 23.1g total fat (13.9g saturated fat); 1327kJ (317 cal); 22.1g carbohydrate; 5.5g protein; 1.3g fibre

tip You can also make individual tiramisu. Cut biscuits in half or thirds (depending on the size of the base of your glasses). Pour ¾ cup of strawberry sauce into a small bowl; dip biscuits into sauce. Place soaked biscuits into bases of six ¾-cup (180ml) glasses. Divide mascarpone mixture among glasses. Cover; refrigerate 1 hour. Refrigerate remaining strawberry sauce. Just before serving, pour remaining strawberry sauce into each glass. Serve topped with small strawberries.

TO REMOVE SEEDS FROM A POMEGRANATE, CUT THE FRUIT IN HALF CROSSWAYS; HOLD ONE HALF AT A TIME, CUT-SIDE DOWN, IN THE PALM OF YOUR HAND OVER A BOWL, THEN HIT THE OUTSIDE FIRMLY WITH A WOODEN SPOON. THE SEEDS SHOULD FALL OUT EASILY; DISCARD ANY WHITE PITH THAT FALLS OUT WITH THEM.

MIDDLE-EASTERN STYLE FRUIT SALAD

3 medium navel oranges (720g)

10 cardamom pods

¾ cup (165g) caster (superfine) sugar

1½ cups (375ml) water

1 vanilla bean, split lengthways, seeds scraped

1 large carrot (180g), cut into matchsticks

1 pomegranate (450g)

3 medium blood oranges (720g)

5 medium peaches (750g), halved, stones removed, cut into wedges

½ cup (125ml) freshly-squeezed orange juice

⅓ cup (80ml) freshly-squeezed lemon juice

1 Using a vegetable peeler, peel rind from one navel orange. Place rind in a small saucepan with cardamom, sugar, the water and vanilla seeds and bean; stir over low heat until sugar dissolves.

2 Add carrot to pan and increase heat to medium; cook 20 minutes or until syrup is thick and carrot is translucent. Using a fork, transfer candied carrot to a small bowl. Transfer unstrained syrup to a large bowl.

3 Remove seeds from pomegranate; reserve seeds. Using a small sharp knife, remove rind and pith from navel and blood oranges, following the curve of the fruit. Cut oranges into 5mm (¼-inch) thick rounds; add to the syrup with pomegranate seeds and peaches. Add juices to bowl; stir to combine.

4 Stir half the candied carrot into fruit salad; divide fruit salad among small bowls. Serve fruit salad topped with remaining candied carrot.

prep + cook time 30 minutes **serves** 6

nutritional count per serving 0.4g total fat (0g saturated fat); 1172kJ (280 cal); 59.8g carbohydrate; 4.1g protein; 11g fibre

tip You will need about 2 extra navel oranges and 2 lemons for the juice in this recipe.

FENNEL
BEETROOT
PERSIMMON
PUMPKIN
POMEGRANATE
MUSHROOMS
EGGPLANT
AUTUMN
PURPLE CARROTS
RED GRAPES
PISTACHIOS
FIGS
RHUBARB
RADICCHIO

VEGETABLES

The autumn harvest sees pumpkin at its best,
as well as carrots, fennel, beetroot and eggplant.
The perfect produce as the weather starts to cool
for oven-roasted vegies and soothing soups.

FRUIT

Autumn fruits are robust, dependable and fragrant.
Juicy ripe pears, perfect plums, fleshy figs and
gorgeous grapes are at their best. Eat them as nature
intended or cook them in one of our creations.

PERSIAN QUAIL, FIG & POMEGRANATE SALAD

1 shallot (25g), chopped finely

1 teaspoon sumac

½ teaspoon ground cinnamon

pinch of caster (superfine) sugar

1 tablespoon pomegranate molasses

⅓ cup (80ml) extra virgin olive oil

4 x 200g (6½-ounce) jumbo quails,
  butterflied (see tips)

¼ cup (60ml) olive oil

1 piece lebanese bread (80g)

1 medium radicchio (200g),
  outer leaves discarded

½ cup loosely packed fresh basil leaves

¼ cup loosely packed fresh
  flat-leaf parsley

½ cup (50g) walnut halves, roasted

6 ripe green figs (400g), sliced thickly

120g (4 ounces) fetta, crumbled

½ pomegranate (225g), seeds removed
  (see tips)

1 Preheat oven to 180°C/350°F.

2 Combine shallot, sumac, cinnamon, sugar, pomegranate molasses and extra virgin olive oil in a small bowl; season. Place quail in a glass or ceramic bowl with half the dressing; toss to coat well. Cover; refrigerate 4 hours or overnight.

3 Heat 2 tablespoons of the olive oil in a heavy-based frying pan over medium heat; cook quail, in batches, skin-side down, for 4 minutes or until golden. Transfer quail, skin-side up, to an oven tray; roast 5 minutes or until breast meat is still slightly pink. Remove from heat; rest 10 minutes. Cut each quail in half along the breastbone, then in half again between legs and breasts to give four pieces.

4 Lightly brush bread on each side with remaining olive oil, place on an oven tray; bake 8 minutes or until crisp and golden. Cool, then break into large pieces.

5 Tear radicchio leaves into large pieces. Place radicchio in a large bowl with herbs, nuts, figs, fetta, pomegranate seeds, remaining dressing and quail; toss gently to combine. Serve immediately with toasted bread.

prep + cook time 45 minutes (+ refrigeration) **serves** 4

nutritional count per serving 59g total fat (13.6g saturated fat); 3462kJ (827 cal); 27.9g carbohydrate; 43.1g protein; 7.7g fibre

tips The technique to split open and flatten quail so that it cooks quickly and evenly is called 'butterflying'. Place quail, breast-side down, on a chopping board. Using poultry shears or kitchen scissors, cut down both sides of the backbone; discard the bone. Turn over, open out and press down on the breast plate to flatten further. Tuck the wings underneath. To remove seeds from a pomegranate, cut the fruit in half crossways; hold the half, cut-side down, in the palm of your hand over a bowl, then hit the outside firmly with a wooden spoon. The seeds should fall out easily; discard any white pith that falls out with them.

PUMPKIN ROTOLO WITH SAGE BUTTER SAUCE

You will need two 45cm (18-inch) square pieces of muslin and a wide baking dish large enough to fit both the rotolo.

1.2kg (2½ pounds) butternut pumpkin, peeled, chopped coarsely

6 cloves garlic, unpeeled

2 tablespoons olive oil

120g (4 ounces) baby spinach

400g (12½ ounces) fresh ricotta

½ cup (40g) finely grated parmesan

1 egg, beaten lightly

4 fresh lasagne sheets (185g)

125g (4 ounces) butter, chopped

12 fresh sage leaves

1 Preheat oven to 200°C/400°F. Place pumpkin and garlic on two oven trays; drizzle with oil, season. Roast 30 minutes or until golden and tender. When cool enough to handle, squeeze garlic from skins; discard skins.

2 Meanwhile, boil, steam or microwave spinach until wilted; drain. Cool. Using your hands, squeeze excess water from spinach; chop coarsely. Place pumpkin, spinach, ricotta, parmesan and egg in a large bowl; stir, mashing pumpkin pieces slightly, until combined. Season to taste.

3 Place two pasta sheets, one above the other with the long sides slightly overlapping, on a 45cm (18-inch) square piece of muslin. Spoon one-quarter of the pumpkin mixture along the long side in front of you, to form a smooth log (this ensures the centre of rotolo is plump). Spread another quarter of the pumpkin mixture over the rest of the pasta, leaving a 3cm (1¼-inch) border at the opposite long side. Using the muslin as a guide, and starting from the long side closest to you, carefully roll up the rotolo to enclose the filling. Wrap rotolo in the muslin, tie a knot at each end and secure with kitchen string at 5cm (2-inch) intervals. Don't tie too tightly as rotolo will expand slightly during cooking. Repeat with remaining pasta sheets, pumpkin mixture and another square of muslin.

4 Bring a deep, large flameproof baking dish or fish kettle of salted water to the boil over high heat. Reduce heat to medium. Carefully lower rolls into water; simmer, uncovered, 20 minutes or until pasta is cooked (rolls will feel firmer). Remove rolls from water; stand 2 minutes.

5 Meanwhile, heat butter in a medium frying pan over medium-high heat; cook 2 minutes or until golden brown. Add sage; cook 30 seconds or until crisp. Remove from heat.

6 Unwrap rotolo; discard muslin. Trim ends, then cut each rotolo into six thick slices. Divide slices among plates; serve drizzled with sage butter sauce.

prep + cook time 2 hours 10 minutes **serves** 4

nutritional count per serving 47.4g total fat (25.4g saturated fat); 2805kJ (670 cal); 37.4g carbohydrate; 20.8g protein; 8.9g fibre

You CAN MAKE THE FILLING UP TO A DAY AHEAD; STORE, COVERED, IN THE REFRIGERATOR UNTIL READY TO USE. UNBAKED EMPANADAS CAN BE FROZEN FOR UP TO 2 MONTHS. BAKE THEM FROM FROZEN FOR 40 MINUTES OR UNTIL GOLDEN.

SPICY PUMPKIN EMPANADAS

580g (1¼-pound) butternut pumpkin, peeled, chopped coarsely

2 tablespoons olive oil

2 tablespoons finely chopped fresh flat-leaf parsley

2 tablespoons finely chopped fresh coriander (cilantro)

2 teaspoons ground cumin

¼ teaspoon cayenne pepper

1 teaspoon ground coriander

1 small red onion (80g), chopped finely

⅔ cup (130g) greek fetta, crumbled

1 egg, beaten lightly

DOUGH

1½ cups (375ml) water

2 teaspoons (7g) dried yeast

1 teaspoon caster (superfine) sugar

4 cups (600g) plain (all-purpose) flour

2 teaspoons fine salt

¼ cup (60ml) olive oil

1 Make dough.

2 Preheat oven to 200°C/400°F. Line two oven trays with baking paper.

3 Meanwhile, combine pumpkin and oil in a large roasting pan; season. Roast, turning occasionally, 20 minutes or until pumpkin is tender. Transfer pumpkin to a heatproof bowl; mash. Stir in herbs, spices, onion and fetta; season to taste. Refrigerate until cooled.

4 Divide dough into 20 balls. Roll each ball on a floured surface into a 10cm (4-inch) round. Spoon 1 rounded tablespoon of the filling mixture onto half of each round; brush edge with a little egg, fold over tightly to enclose filling and form a half-moon shape. Twist the edge to seal filling (or crimp with a floured fork); place on trays. Brush tops with a little more egg.

5 Bake empanadas 30 minutes or until golden. Serve hot or at room temperature.

dough Combine the water, yeast and sugar in a small bowl. Set aside for 5 minutes or until foamy. Combine flour and salt in a large bowl; make a well in the centre. Add yeast mixture and oil. Using your hands, mix until combined. Turn dough onto a floured surface; knead 10 minutes or until smooth and elastic. Place dough in an oiled large bowl; turn to coat in oil. Cover with plastic wrap; set aside in a warm, draught-free place for 1 hour or until dough doubles in size.

prep + cook time 1 hour 30 minutes (+ standing) **makes** 20

nutritional count per empanada 6.8g total fat (1.8g saturated fat); 755kJ (180 cal); 23.8g carbohydrate; 15.1g protein; 1.8g fibre

serving suggestion Serve with a chunky Mexican tomato salsa.

CHICKEN, MUSHROOM & FENNEL PIES

1 tablespoon olive oil

2 cloves garlic, crushed

1 medium leek (350g), sliced thinly

1 small fennel bulb (200g),
    sliced thinly

200g (6½ ounces) swiss brown
    mushrooms, quartered

½ cup (125ml) dry white wine

4 chicken breast fillets (800g),
    chopped coarsely

300ml pouring cream

1 tablespoon dijon mustard

¼ cup coarsely chopped
    fresh flat-leaf parsley

2 sheets puff pastry

1 egg, beaten lightly

1 tablespoon fennel seeds

½ teaspoon sea salt flakes

1 Preheat oven to 200°C/400°F.

2 Heat oil in a large saucepan over medium heat; cook garlic, leek, fennel and mushrooms, stirring, for 5 minutes or until vegetables soften.

3 Stir in wine; bring to the boil. Reduce heat; simmer, 3 minutes. Add chicken and cream; bring to the boil. Reduce heat; simmer 10 minutes or until chicken is cooked through and sauce has thickened slightly. Stir in mustard and parsley.

4 Spoon filling into four 1½ cup (375ml) ovenproof bowls or dishes. Cut pastry sheets in half; trim halves into 12cm x 18cm (4¾-inch x 7¼-inch) rectangles. Place a pastry rectangle on each bowl, pressing down gently to seal. Brush pastry with egg. Using a small sharp knife, score five lines on each pastry lid at 2.5cm (1-inch) intervals; sprinkle tops wtih fennel seeds and salt.

5 Bake pies for 25 minutes or until pastry is puffed and golden.

prep + cook time 40 minutes **serves** 4

nutritional count per serving 58.9g total fat (32.3g saturated fat); 3989kJ (953 cal); 43.3g carbohydrate; 57.5g protein; 5.2g fibre

serving suggestion Serve with a fresh rocket salad. Place 2 tablespoons lemon juice, 1 tablespoon extra virgin olive oil and a clove of garlic in a screw-top jar; shake well. Place 100g (3 ounces) baby rocket (arugula) leaves in a large bowl with ¼ cup chopped fresh flat-leaf parsley, ¼ cup fresh mint leaves and dressing; toss gently to combine. Serve salad topped with 2 chopped green onions (scallions).

HARISSA EGGPLANT
& CHORIZO SALAD
(RECIPE PAGE 80)

HARISSA EGGPLANT & CHORIZO SALAD

2 x 420g (13½ ounces) canned chickpeas (garbanzo beans), drained, rinsed

½ cup (140g) Greek-style yoghurt

1 large eggplant (500g)

2 tablespoons olive oil

2 cured chorizo sausages (340g), sliced thinly

180g (5½ ounces) bocconcini cheese, torn

1 cup loosely packed fresh basil leaves

HARISSA DRESSING

2 tablespoons red wine vinegar

2 tablespoons olive oil

2 teaspoons harissa paste

1 teaspoon caster (superfine) sugar

1 Make harissa dressing.

2 Process half the chickpeas with yoghurt until smooth. Season to taste.

3 Cut eggplant lengthways into thin slices; place in a medium bowl with oil, toss to coat. Season. Cook eggplant on a heated oiled barbecue (or chargrill plate or grill) for 1½ minutes each side or until tender. Transfer to a plate; cover to keep warm.

4 Meanwhile, cook chorizo on barbecue until browned both sides.

5 Place remaining chickpeas, eggplant and chorizo in a large bowl with bocconcini, basil and dressing; toss gently to combine.

6 Arrange salad on a platter, top with chickpea puree.

harissa dressing Whisk ingredients together in a small bowl. Season to taste.

prep + cook time 30 minutes serves 4

nutritional count per serving 61.4g total fat (21.7g saturated fat); 3610kJ (862 cal); 33.7g carbohydrate; 40.3g protein; 9.8g fibre

(photograph page 79)

SPICED CARROT SOUP WITH SMOKED ALMONDS

1 tablespoon olive oil

2 medium brown onions (300g), chopped coarsely

2 teaspoons finely grated fresh ginger

2 teaspoons ground cumin

1 teaspoon ground coriander

½ cinnamon stick

1kg (2 pounds) carrots, chopped coarsely

2 cups (500ml) vegetable stock

3 cups (750ml) water

¾ cup (200g) Greek-style yoghurt

2 cloves garlic, crushed

½ small red onion (50g), sliced thinly

¼ cup (40g) chopped smoked almonds

1 Heat oil in a large saucepan over medium heat; cook brown onion, stirring, for 8 minutes or until soft.

2 Add ginger, cumin, ground coriander and cinnamon to pan; cook, stirring, until fragrant. Add carrot, stock and the water; bring to the boil. Reduce heat; simmer, covered, 20 minutes or until soft. Remove cinnamon stick. Stand soup 10 minutes.

3 Meanwhile, combine yoghurt and garlic in a small bowl.

4 Blend soup in batches until smooth (or use a stick blender). Return soup to pan; stir over medium heat until hot. Season.

5 Ladle soup into bowls; top with yoghurt mixture, red onion and nuts.

prep + cook time 45 minutes serves 4

nutritional count per serving 14.5g total fat (3.3g saturated fat); 1190kJ (284 cal); 24g carbohydrate; 8.9g protein; 11.7g fibre

SPICED CARROT SOUP
WITH SMOKED ALMONDS

TRY USING A VARIETY OF MUSHROOMS SUCH AS FLAT, CUP, BUTTON, PORTOBELLO, OYSTER AND ENOKI, KEEPING SMALL MUSHROOMS HALVED OR WHOLE AND LARGE TYPES SLICED. COOKING THE POTATOES WHOLE WITH THE PEEL ON KEEPS THE POTATOES DRY AND FLUFFY — DOING THIS HELPS TO CREATE LIGHTLY TEXTURED PILLOWS OF GNOCCHI.

POTATO GNOCCHI WITH MUSHROOMS & THYME

2 tablespoons olive oil

375g (12 ounces) assorted mushrooms, sliced thinly (see note above)

2 teaspoons finely chopped fresh lemon thyme

2 cloves garlic, crushed

300ml pouring cream

⅓ cup (25g) finely grated parmesan

2 teaspoons fresh lemon thyme sprigs, extra

POTATO GNOCCHI

500g (1 pound) desiree potatoes, unpeeled

1 egg, beaten lightly

15g (½ ounce) butter, melted

2 tablespoons finely grated parmesan

1 cup (150g) plain (all-purpose) flour, approximately

1 Make potato gnocchi.

2 Heat oil in a large frying pan over high heat; cook mushrooms and thyme, allowing the mushrooms to brown well before turning occasionally, for 5 minutes or until golden. Add garlic; stir 30 seconds or until softened. Add cream; bring to the boil. Reduce heat; simmer, uncovered, until sauce thickens. Stir in half the parmesan. Season to taste.

3 Meanwhile, cook gnocchi, in batches, in a large saucepan of boiling water until gnocchi float to the surface and are cooked through. Remove from pan with a slotted spoon to a bowl; cover keep warm.

4 Once all gnocchi are cooked, add to mushroom sauce; stir gently. Serve topped with remaining parmesan and extra thyme sprigs.

potato gnocchi Boil whole potatoes until tender; drain. When cool enough to handle, peel away skins. Mash potatoes, using a ricer or potato masher into a medium bowl; stir in egg, butter, parmesan and enough flour to make a firm dough. Divide dough into four portions; roll each portion on a floured surface into 2cm (¾-inch) thick ropes. Cut each rope into 2cm (¾-inch) pieces. Place gnocchi, in a single layer, on a lightly floured tray; cover refrigerate 1 hour.

prep + cook time 1 hour (+ refrigeration) **serves** 4

nutritional count per serving 44g total fat (23.3g saturated fat); 2761kJ (680 cal); 46.3g carbohydrate; 17.1g protein; 6g fibre

COLOURFUL HEIRLOOM CARROTS, IN HUES OF PURPLE, TASTE THE SAME AS THEIR ORANGE COUSINS, AND WERE IN FACT THE NORM, UNTIL THE DUTCH DEVELOPED THE MODERN-DAY ORANGE CULTIVATORS IN THE 17TH CENTURY.

BEETROOT & HEIRLOOM CARROT SALAD WITH PERSIAN FETTA

500g (1 pound) golden baby beetroot (beets), trimmed

500g (1 pounds) red baby beetroot (beets), trimmed

800g (1½ pounds) baby carrots, trimmed

800g (1½ pounds) baby purple carrots, trimmed

1 large red onion (300g), cut into thick wedges

2 teaspoons dijon mustard

½ cup loosely packed fresh mint leaves

180g (5½-ounce) tub persian fetta, drained, crumbled

DRESSING

½ cup (125ml) olive oil

¼ cup (60ml) red wine vinegar

1 tablespoon honey

1 Make dressing.

2 Preheat oven to 200°C/400°F. Line two oven trays with baking paper.

3 Scrub beetroot and carrots. Divide beetroot, carrot and onion between trays. Spoon half the dressing over vegetables; toss to coat. Season. Roast 45 minutes or until vegetables are tender; cool slightly. Peel beetroot; cut in half (or quarters if large). Cut carrots in half lengthways.

4 Stir mustard into remaining dressing.

5 Arrange vegetables on a platter; top with mint and remaining dressing. Serve warm topped wtih fetta.

dressing Whisk ingredients together in a small bowl; season to taste.

prep + cook time 1 hour serves 8

nutritional count per serving 14.6g total fat (2.3g saturated fat); 1068kJ (255 cal); 21.9g carbohydrate; 4g protein; 11.6g fibre

tip Orange carrots are known for their beta carotene content, while purple ones contain the purple pigment anthocyanin, a powerful antioxidant. Carrots share the same botanical family as parsnips, fennel and parsley, vegetables and herbs that they also partner well with in the kitchen.

KUMARA & GOAT'S CHEESE TART

1 medium kumara (orange sweet
   potato) (400g), diced

1 tablespoon olive oil

3 eggs

⅔ cup (160ml) pouring cream

⅓ cup (25g) finely grated parmesan

100g (3 ounces) soft goat's cheese,
   crumbled

125g (4 ounces) mixed baby
   salad leaves

2 shallots (50g), sliced thinly

½ cup (75g) drained semi-dried
   tomatoes, chopped coarsely

⅓ cup (25g) shaved parmesan

1½ tablespoons olive oil

2 tablespoons lemon juice

PASTRY

1½ cups (225g) plain (all-purpose) flour

1 tablespoon fresh thyme leaves

125g (4 ounces) cold butter, chopped

1 egg yolk

2 tablespoons chilled water

1 Preheat oven to 200°C/400°F. Place kumara on an oven tray; drizzle with oil. Roast 30 minutes or until tender.

2 Meanwhile, make pastry.

3 Roll pastry between sheets of baking paper until large enough to line a 24cm (9½-inch) round loose-based tart tin. Lift pastry into tin, press into side, trim edge; prick base all over with fork. Cover; refrigerate 20 minutes.

4 Reduce oven to 190°C/375°F.

5 Place tin on an oven tray; line with baking paper then fill with dried beans or rice. Bake 15 minutes. Remove paper and beans; bake a further 10 minutes or until browned lightly. Cool on tray.

6 Whisk eggs, cream and parmesan in a medium jug until combined. Season. Place kumara in pastry case; pour in egg mixture. Top with goat's cheese.

7 Bake tart 35 minutes or until just set.

8 Place salad leaves, shallots, tomatoes, parmesan, oil and juice in a medium bowl; toss gently to combine. Season to taste.

9 Serve tart topped with salad.

pastry Process flour, thyme and butter until crumbly. Add egg yolk and the water; process until ingredients come together. Wrap in plastic wrap; refrigerate 30 minutes.

prep + cook time 1 hour 25 minutes (+ refrigeration) serves 6

nutritional count per serving 44.5g total fat (23.5g saturated fat); 2693kJ (643 cal); 41.4g carbohydrate; 17.9g protein; 4.9g fibre

tips We used baby kale leaves, available from selected supermarkets, but you could also use watercress or your favourite mix of baby salad leaves. Kumara can be roasted a day ahead. Pastry case can be made a day ahead. You can also make six individual tarts in 3cm (1¼-inch) deep, 10cm (4-inch) round loose-based tart tins; bake for 25 minutes.

FOR A CONTRASTING TEXTURE, TOP THE PASTA WITH A LITTLE SHAVED RAW PEAR.
WHILE THIS RECIPE IS GEARED FOR AUTUMN, YOU CAN SWAP INGREDIENTS FOR
THE SEASONS. IN SPRING, USE BROAD BEANS INSTEAD OF BORLOTTI BEANS
AND BITTER SALAD GREENS INSTEAD OF THE RADICCHIO.

PASTA WITH NUT PASTE, PEAR & BORLOTTI BEANS

600g (1¼ pounds) fresh borlotti
    beans, shelled

½ cup (80g) blanched almonds,
    roasted

½ cup (50g) walnuts, roasted

1 clove garlic, crushed

¼ cup firmly packed fresh flat-leaf
    parsley, chopped coarsely

½ teaspoon freshly ground
    black pepper

½ cup (125ml) olive oil

375g (13 ounces) penne pasta

2 medium pears (460g), unpeeled,
    cut into thin wedges

1 tablespoon olive oil, extra

1 medium radicchio (200g),
    leaves separated, torn

120g (4 ounces) blue cheese, crumbled

¼ cup loosely packed fresh
    flat-leaf parsley sprigs, extra

1 Place borlotti beans in a large saucepan of cold water. Bring to the boil; boil 25 minutes or until tender. Drain.

2 Process nuts, garlic, parsley and pepper until finely chopped. With the motor operating, gradually pour in ¼ cup of the oil until combined. Season with salt.

3 Cook pasta in a large saucepan of boiling salted water 8 minutes or until almost tender. Drain; reserving ½ cup of the cooking water. Return pasta to pan; cover to keep warm.

4 Meanwhile, season pears. Heat extra oil in a large frying pan over medium heat; cook pear for 2 minutes each side or until golden. Drain on paper towel. Add beans to same pan, stirring for 2 minutes or until heated through.

5 Add nut paste to pasta with enough reserved cooking water for the paste to coat the pasta (do not return the pan to the heat or the nut paste will thicken and make the mixture dry). Add pears, beans and radicchio; toss gently to combine. Season.

6 Serve pasta topped with cheese and parsley sprigs, drizzled with remaining oil.

prep + cook time 40 minutes **serves** 4

nutritional count per serving 64.7g total fat (13g saturated fat); 4640kJ (1108 cal); 98g carbohydrate; 29.4g protein; 10.7g fibre

FOR THE BEST FLAVOUR, ENSURE MUSHROOMS ARE BROWNED WELL. USE A HEAVY-BASED FRYING PAN AND AVOID MOVING THE MUSHROOMS AROUND TOO MUCH WHILE THEY'RE COOKING - ALLOW THEM TO CATCH AND BROWN BEFORE STIRRING. IF YOU DON'T HAVE A HEAVY-BASED PAN, HEAT THE PAN FIRST BEFORE ADDING THE OIL AND BUTTER.

FREE-FORM MUSHROOM & CHEESE TART

60g (2 ounces) butter

2 tablespoons olive oil

400g (12 ounces) swiss brown mushrooms, sliced thinly

400g (12 ounces) button mushrooms, sliced thinly

2 shallots (50g), chopped finely

200g (6½ ounces) spring onion and chive cream cheese

2 eggs

½ cup (40g) finely grated parmesan

¼ cup coarsely chopped fresh flat-leaf parsley

2 sheets puff pastry

1 egg, extra, beaten lightly

100g (3 ounces) fresh ricotta, crumbled coarsely (see tips)

12 small fresh thyme sprigs

½ cup (120g) smooth packaged ricotta (see tips)

¼ cup loosely packed fresh flat-leaf parsley sprigs

1 Preheat oven to 220°C/425°F. Line two oven trays with baking paper.

2 Heat half the butter and half the oil in a large heavy-based frying pan over high heat. Add half the mushrooms and half the shallots; season. Cook, stirring occasionally, 4 minutes or until mushrooms are golden. Transfer to a medium bowl. Repeat with remaining butter, oil, mushrooms and shallots.

3 Meanwhile, process cream cheese, eggs and parmesan until smooth.

4 Place a pastry sheet on each oven tray. Spread cream cheese mixture evenly between sheets, into a 16cm (6½-inch) round, leaving a 4cm (1½-inch) border; top with mushroom mixture and chopped parsley. Brush the border with a little of the extra egg. Fold in pastry corners, then remaining sides to partially cover the filling and create a rim. Brush pastry rim with a little more egg. Sprinkle crumbled ricotta and thyme over filling.

5 Bake tarts for 15 minutes or until pastry is puffed and golden. Serve tarts topped with spoonfuls of smooth ricotta and parsley sprigs.

prep + cook time 1 hour **serves** 4

nutritional count per serving 62.3g total fat (33g saturated fat); 3696kJ (833 cal); 46.4g carbohydrate; 31g protein; 6.6g fibre

tips You will need to buy two types or ricotta for this recipe: use fresh, dry ricotta, cut from a wheel from the deli counter to crumble over the tart before cooking, and the smooth variety sold in tubs to spoon on the tart just before serving.

You can use a garlic and herb flavoured cream cheese instead of the spring onion and chive flavour if you prefer.

MOROCCAN CHICKPEAS & CARROTS
WITH SPINACH COUSCOUS
(RECIPE PAGE 94)

MOROCCAN CHICKPEAS & CARROTS WITH SPINACH COUSCOUS

10 baby carrots (200g)

1 tablespoon olive oil

2 teaspoons ground cumin

1 teaspoon sweet paprika

1 teaspoon caster (superfine) sugar

½ cup (125ml) water

1¼ cups (250g) couscous

1¼ cups (310ml) boiling water

30g (1 ounce) butter, chopped

400g (12½ ounces) canned chickpeas (garbanzo beans), drained, rinsed

1 tablespoon lemon juice

50g (1½ ounces) baby spinach leaves, shredded

1 cup loosely packed fresh mint leaves

1 Trim and peel carrots, leaving 3cm (1¼ inches) of the stem; halve lengthways.

2 Heat oil in a medium saucepan over medium heat; cook spices 30 seconds or until fragrant. Add carrots, sugar and the water; season to taste. Bring to the boil; simmer, partially covered, for 12 minutes or until carrots are tender.

3 Meanwhile, combine couscous with the boiling water in a large heatproof bowl. Cover; stand 10 minutes. Fluff with a fork. Stir in butter; season to taste.

4 Add chickpeas to pan; cook, covered, 3 minutes or until heated through. Stir in juice.

5 Stir spinach through couscous; spoon onto a platter. Top with carrot mixture and mint.

prep + cook time 30 minutes **serves** 4

nutritional count per serving 12.4g total fat (4.8g saturated fat); 1682kJ (402 cal); 56.7g carbohydrate; 11.4g protein; 8g fibre

serving suggestion Serve with Greek-style yoghurt and harissa.

(photograph page 92)

PUMPKIN BRUSCHETTA WITH ALMOND SKORDALIA

500g (1 pound) jap pumpkin, unpeeled

2 tablespoons olive oil

8 thin slices sourdough bread (200g)

100g (3 ounces) fetta, crumbled

½ cup loosely packed fresh flat-leaf parsley leaves

2 tablespoons olive oil, extra

ALMOND SKORDALIA

1 cup (160g) blanched almonds

2 cloves garlic, crushed

1 cup (70g) coarsely chopped day-old bread

2 tablespoons white wine vinegar

⅓ cup (80ml) olive oil

½ cup (125ml) water

1 Make almond skordalia.

2 Cut pumpkin into thin wedges. Place pumpkin and half the oil in a large bowl; toss to coat. Season. Cook pumpkin on a heated oiled barbecue (or chargrill plate or grill) for 4 minutes each side or until tender.

3 Brush bread with remaining oil; place bread on heated oiled barbecue until browned both sides.

4 Spread chargrilled bread with almond skordalia. Top with pumpkin, fetta and parsley; drizzle with extra oil.

almond skordalia Toast nuts in a medium frying pan, stirring occasionally, until browned lightly. Cool. Process nuts, garlic, bread and vinegar until wet breadcrumbs form. With motor operating, gradually add oil in a thin, steady stream; add the water, processing until smooth. Season to taste.

prep + cook time 30 minutes **serves** 8

nutritional count per serving 32.7g total fat (6g saturated fat); 1832kJ (438 cal); 25.6g carbohydrate; 11.6g protein; 3.2g fibre

PUMPKIN BRUSCHETTA
WITH ALMOND SKORDALIA

IF ROASTED HAZELNUTS ARE UNAVAILABLE, YOU CAN ROAST YOUR OWN. PLACE NUTS ON AN OVEN TRAY; ROAST AT 200°C/400°F FOR 5 MINUTES OR UNTIL THE SKINS BEGIN TO SPLIT. PLACE NUTS IN A TEA TOWEL AND RUB THEM TOGETHER TO REMOVE THE SKIN. LEAVE TO COOL. IF THE LEAVES ON YOUR BEETROOT ARE FRESH, YOU CAN TRIM, WASH AND RESERVE THE SMALLEST ONES, THEN ADD TO THE SALAD WITH THE WATERCRESS.

BABY BEETROOT, LENTIL & WATERCRESS SALAD

1kg (2 pounds) baby beetroot (beets)

2 cloves garlic, sliced

¼ cup fresh rosemary leaves

2 tablespoons extra virgin olive oil

¼ cup (60ml) balsamic vinegar

½ cup (100g) French-style green lentils

1 large pomegranate (430g)

3 cups (90g) trimmed watercress

⅓ cup (45g) roasted hazelnuts, halved

1 Preheat oven to 200°C/400°F.

2 Trim beetroot tops to 4cm (1½ inches); halve beetroot, or quarter if large. Place beetroot, garlic and rosemary in a large ovenproof dish; drizzle with oil and vinegar. Roast, uncovered, 30 minutes or until tender.

3 Meanwhile, cook lentils in a medium saucepan of boiling water for 25 minutes or until lentils are tender. Drain; rinse under cold water. Drain well.

4 Cut pomegranate in half crossways; hold a half, cut-side down, in the palm of your hand over a small bowl, then hit the outside firmly with a wooden spoon. The seeds should fall out easily; discard any white pith that falls out with them. Repeat with the other half.

5 Place lentils, beetroot and cooking juices, watercress, half the pomegranate seeds and half the nuts in a large bowl; toss gently to combine. Season to taste. Transfer to a serving bowl; top with remaining pomegranate seeds and nuts.

prep + cook time 40 minutes serves 4

nutritional count per serving 16.9g total fat (1.9g saturated fat); 1605kJ (383 cal); 36.4g carbohydrate; 13.4g protein; 17.1g fibre

tips If you would like to add meat to the salad, cook 2 x 220g (7-ounce) new york steaks on a heated oiled barbecue (or chargrill plate) for 2 minutes each side for medium rare or until cooked as desired. Cover and rest 5 minutes; slice thinly, then toss through the salad.

When the days begin to shorten and the leaves change colour, you know that autumn is here. Outdoor types relish the milder weather, sharing cook-ups on the campfire and memories of the good old days.

SPICED PUMPKIN & HONEY PIES

1½ cups (225g) plain (all-purpose) flour

125g (4 ounces) cold butter, chopped

2 tablespoons icing (confectioners') sugar

1 egg yolk

1 tablespoon chilled water

1 egg yolk, extra

½ cup (125ml) thick (double) cream

3 teaspoons honey

¼ cup (25g) coarsely chopped walnuts

SPICED PUMPKIN FILLING

1kg (2 pounds) jap or butternut pumpkin, chopped coarsely

pinch of sea salt

¾ teaspoon ground ginger

½ teaspoon ground cinnamon

2 eggs

2 tablespoons milk

¼ cup (90g) honey

2 tablespoons caster (superfine) sugar

1 Process flour, butter and sugar until mixture resembles breadcrumbs. Add egg yolk and the water; process until ingredients come together. Divide pastry into six portions, wrap each in plastic wrap; refrigerate 30 minutes.

2 Meanwhile, make spiced pumpkin filling.

3 Roll pastry between sheets of baking paper until large enough to line six 10cm (4-inch) round, 3cm (1¼-inch) deep, loose-based tart tins. Lift pastry into tins, press into base and sides, trim edge; prick bases all over with fork. Cover; refrigerate for 20 minutes.

4 Meanwhile, preheat oven to 180°C/350°F.

5 Place tins on an oven tray; line each with baking paper, fill with dried beans or rice. Bake 15 minutes. Remove paper and beans; bake a further 10 minutes or until browned lightly. Cool on tray.

6 Spoon pumpkin filling into pastry cases. Brush tops with extra egg yolk. Bake pies 25 minutes or until set and light golden.

7 Just before serving, spoon cream onto pies, drizzle with honey and top with nuts.

spiced pumpkin filling Boil, steam or microwave pumpkin until just tender; drain. Process pumpkin, salt, ginger and cinnamon until smooth. Add eggs, milk, honey and sugar; process until smooth. Cool.

prep + cook time 1 hour 45 minutes (+ refrigeration & cooling) **makes** 6

nutritional count per pie 34.5g total fat (19g saturated fat); 2616kJ (625 cal); 66.6g carbohydrate; 11g protein; 6.2g fibre

tip The pies can be made a day ahead. Before serving, reheat in a 160°C/325°F oven for 10 minutes or until warm.

WHILE RHUBARB IS GENERALLY AVAILABLE YEAR-ROUND, SUPPLIES AND QUALITY ARE MORE ABUNDANT IN THE COOLER MONTHS OF AUTUMN. RHUBARB IS GENERALLY REGARDED AS A FRUIT, HOWEVER TECHNICALLY IT IS A VEGETABLE AND PAIRS WELL WITH RICH MEATS.

RHUBARB & CUSTARD BREAD PUDDING

1¾ cups (430ml) pouring cream

1½ cups (375ml) milk

1 vanilla bean, split lengthways

700g (1½-pound) loaf sliced white bread, crusts removed

60g (2 ounces) butter, softened

6 eggs

¾ cup (165g) caster (superfine) sugar

20g (¾ ounce) butter, melted, extra

2 tablespoons demerara sugar

1 tablespoon icing (confectioners') sugar

RHUBARB & RASPBERRY JAM

700g (1½ pounds) trimmed rhubarb, chopped coarsely

½ cup (110g) caster (superfine) sugar

⅓ cup (80ml) water

⅔ cup (100g) frozen raspberries

1 Make rhubarb and raspberry jam.

2 Preheat oven to 160°C/325°F. Grease a 2-litre (8-cup) baking dish measuring 24cm x 34cm x 5cm (9½-inch x 13½-inch x 2-inch).

3 Place cream, milk and vanilla bean in a medium saucepan over medium heat. Bring to a simmer; stand 15 minutes. Discard vanilla bean.

4 Meanwhile, spread bread slices with softened butter, flattening the bread slightly (this will help it stay rolled when filled). Spread slices with tablespoons of jam. Roll slices up like a swiss roll to enclose filling; cut in half crossways. Arrange bread spirals, cut-side up, in dish.

5 Whisk eggs and caster sugar in a large bowl until combined; whisk in cream mixture. Pour custard mixture over bread; stand 15 minutes.

6 Brush tops of bread spirals with melted butter; sprinkle with demerara sugar.

7 Bake pudding for 40 minutes or until custard is just set; stand 10 minutes before serving, dusted with icing sugar.

rhubarb & raspberry jam Place ingredients in a large saucepan over medium heat; bring to a simmer. Simmer, uncovered, 15 minutes or until thick. Cool.

prep + cook time 1 hour 30 minutes (+ cooling & standing) serves 8

nutritional count per serving 33.7g total fat (20g saturated fat); 2671kJ (638 cal); 68.5g carbohydrate; 14.6g protein; 4.4g fibre

tips You will need about 1 large bunch of rhubarb for this recipe. To test when the pudding is cooked, insert a small sharp knife into the centre then withdraw the blade. If the blade is clean, the pudding is ready.

serving suggestion Serve with custard or thick (double) cream.

TO PREVENT THE FILLO PASTRY FROM DRYING OUT WHILE YOU'RE NOT USING IT, KEEP IT COVERED WITH A LAYER OF PLASTIC WRAP, THEN A DAMP TEA TOWEL.

PISTACHIO, WALNUT & CHOCOLATE BAKLAVA

12 sheets fillo pastry

120g (4 ounces) butter, melted

2 tablespoons finely chopped walnuts

FILLING

1½ cups (210g) pistachios

2 cups (200g) walnuts

200g (6 ounces) dark (semi-sweet) chocolate, chopped coarsely

⅓ cup (75g) caster (superfine) sugar

2 teaspoons ground cinnamon

1½ tablespoons finely grated orange rind

HONEY SYRUP

1½ cup (330g) caster (superfine) sugar

1½ cup (375ml) water

½ cup (175g) honey

1 medium orange (240g), rind peeled in long strips

⅓ cup (80ml) orange juice

1 Preheat oven to 190°C/375°F. Grease a 22cm x 40cm x 2.5cm (9-inch x 16-inch x 1-inch) oven tray, then line with baking paper.

2 Make filling.

3 Layer three pastry sheets, brushing each with a little of the butter. Spread half the filling over pastry, leaving a 3cm (1¼-inch) border along both long sides. Starting at one long side, roll up pastry to form a log. Place log on oven tray, brush with butter. Repeat with remaining pastry, butter and filling.

4 Bake baklava 20 minutes or until golden.

5 Meanwhile, make honey syrup.

6 Stand baklava in tray for 5 minutes to cool slightly. Using a small sharp knife, cut each log, on the diagonal, into nine 2cm (¾-inch) wide pieces in the tray. Pour hot syrup over baklava; stand 3 hours or until syrup is absorbed. Serve topped with chopped walnuts.

filling Place nuts on an oven tray; roast in oven 5 minutes or until browned lightly. Cool completely. Process nuts with remaining ingredients until finely chopped.

honey syrup Stir sugar, the water, honey and rind in a small saucepan, over medium heat, without boiling, until sugar dissolves. Bring to a simmer. Simmer 20 minutes or until thickened slightly. Stir in juice.

prep + cook time 1 hour 10 minutes (+ cooling & standing) **makes** 36
nutritional count per piece 11.5g total fat (3.3g saturated fat); 848kJ (203 cal); 22.4g carbohydrate; 2.8g protein; 1.2g fibre
serving suggestion Serve with Greek-style yoghurt.

PLUM & HAZELNUT CLAFOUTIS
(RECIPE PAGE 108)

PLUM & HAZELNUT CLAFOUTIS

500g (1 pound) red-flesh plums

60g (2 ounces) butter, softened

½ cup (110g) caster (superfine) sugar

4 eggs

½ cup (60g) ground hazelnuts

300ml pouring cream

¼ cup (70g) roasted skinless hazelnuts, halved

1½ teaspoons icing (confectioners') sugar

1 Preheat oven to 180°C/350°F.

2 Cut plums in half; remove and discard stones. Place plums, cut-side up, in a greased 1-litre (4-cup) shallow ovenproof dish.

3 Beat butter and sugar in a large bowl with an electric mixer until light and fluffy. Whisk in eggs, one at a time, then whisk in ground hazelnuts and cream until just combined. Pour batter between plums.

4 Bake clafoutis 40 minutes or until golden and a knife inserted in the centre comes out clean.

5 Serve clafoutis warm, topped with hazelnuts and dusted with icing sugar.

prep + cook time 1 hour **serves** 6

nutritional count per serving 42.5g total fat (18.4g saturated fat); 2189kJ (523 cal); 26g carbohydrate; 9.2g protein; 3.6g fibre

serving suggestion Serve with pouring cream or custard.

(photograph page 107)

PERSIMMON MAPLE UPSIDE-DOWN CAKE

1 cup (250ml) maple syrup

220g (7 ounces) unsalted butter, softened, chopped

3 persimmons (fuji) (600g), sliced thinly

1½ cups (330g) caster (superfine) sugar

1 tablespoon finely grated lemon rind

3 eggs, separated

1½ teaspoons vanilla extract

¾ cup (115g) plain (all-purpose) flour

1½ teaspoons baking powder

¾ cup (180ml) milk

1½ cups (270g) fine semolina

¾ cup (100g) coarsely chopped pistachios

2 persimmons (fuji) (400g), extra, sliced

1 Preheat oven to 170°C/340°F. Grease a 24cm (9½-inch) round cake pan; line base with baking paper.

2 Stir syrup and 75g (2½ ounces) of butter in a small saucepan over low heat until butter melts. Increase heat to medium; boil 4 minutes or until mixture thickens. Cool 5 minutes.

3 Pour half the syrup mixture over the base of cake pan (reserve remaining in saucepan); arrange persimmon slices on base of pan.

4 Beat remaining butter with sugar and rind in a medium bowl with an electric mixer for 6 minutes or until pale and fluffy. Beat in egg yolks and extract. Add combined sifted flour and baking powder, and milk; beat on low speed until almost combined. Add semolina; beat until combined.

5 Beat egg whites in another medium bowl with electric mixer until firm peaks form; gently fold into cake mixture. Carefully spread mixture evenly over persimmon; top with nuts.

6 Bake 1 hour 20 minutes or until a skewer inserted into the centre comes out clean. Stand cake in pan for 30 minutes. Run a palette knife around the edge of the cake; turn onto a platter.

7 Add extra persimmon to reserved syrup mixture. Cook over low heat, turning, 5 mintues. Top cake with persimmon mixture.

prep + cook time 2 hours 15 minutes (+ cooling) **serves** 12

nutritional count per serving 21.7g total fat (11.3g saturated fat); 2303kJ (550 cal); 82g carbohydrate; 7.6g protein; 4g fibre

tips We used the firm, non-astringent persimmon variety (fuji fruit) in this recipe. This cake is best made on day of serving.

PERSIMMON MAPLE
UPSIDE-DOWN CAKE

Buy fresh ricotta cut from a wheel, sold at delicatessens or the supermarket deli counter, for the best texture. Pre-packaged ricotta will be too wet for this recipe.

RICOTTA & CHOCOLATE CHEESECAKE WITH GRAPES

1 vanilla bean

750g (1½ pounds) ricotta

½ cup (175g) honey

2 tablespoons caster (superfine) sugar

2 teaspoons finely grated orange rind

3 free-range eggs

150g (4½ ounces) dark chocolate
    (70% cocoa), chopped finely

1½ cups (240g) red and black grapes

1 tablespoon honey, extra

1 Preheat oven to 150°C/300°F. Grease a 22cm (9-inch) springform pan; line base and side with baking paper, extending the paper 3cm (1¼ inches) above the edge.

2 Split vanilla bean in half lengthways; scrape seeds into a large bowl of an electric mixer. Add ricotta, honey, sugar and rind; beat with an electric mixer on medium-high speed 3 minutes or until smooth. Beat in eggs, one at time, until just combined. Stir in chocolate and one-third of the red and black grapes. Pour mixture into pan.

3 Bake cheesecake 55 minutes or until the centre is almost firm to touch. Turn oven off; cool in oven with door ajar. Refrigerate cheesecake for 4 hours or until firm.

4 Just before serving, cut some of the remaining red grapes in half; top cheesecake with all remaining grapes, then drizzle with extra honey.

prep + cook time 1 hour 30 minutes (+ cooling & refrigeration) serves 12

nutritional count per serving 10g total fat (5.7g saturated fat); 977kJ (233 cal); 29.7g carbohydrate; 7.8g protein; 0.7g fibre

tips When chopping the chocolate aim for fairly even pieces about 5mm (¼-inch) in size. Cooling the cheesecake in the oven after it has been turned off, ensures that it will cool slowly and prevent the top from cracking.

EARL GREY MERINGUES WITH SYRUP-SOAKED FIGS

2 earl grey tea bags

1 cup (220g) caster (superfine) sugar

4 egg whites, at room temperature

3 teaspoons cornflour (cornstarch)

1 teaspoon white vinegar

SYRUP-SOAKED FIGS

2 earl grey tea bags

8 long strips orange rind

1 cup (220g) caster (superfine) sugar

½ cup (125ml) water

¼ cup (60ml) fresh orange juice

8 medium figs (480g), sliced thickly

SWEETENED MASCARPONE

500g (1 pound) mascarpone

1 teaspoon vanilla extract

1 tablespoon icing (confectioners')
  sugar

1 Preheat oven to 150°C/300°F. Grease two large oven trays. Mark four 12cm (4¾-inch) rounds on each of two pieces of baking paper; turn paper, marked-side down, onto trays.

2 Remove tea from bags; process with sugar until finely ground.

3 Beat egg whites in a medium bowl with an electric mixer until soft peaks form. Gradually add tea sugar mixture; beat until stiff and glossy. Sift cornflour over meringue, add vinegar; fold in using a metal spoon. Divide mixture among rounds on trays; using a spatula, spread meringue just inside the marked rounds, creating swirls and peaks.

4 Reduce oven to 120°C/250°F; bake meringues 45 minutes or until firm to the touch. Turn oven off; cool in oven with door ajar, for at least 4 hours or overnight. (The tops will crack a little but don't worry they will be covered with cream.)

5 Before serving (about 30 minutes), make syrup-soaked figs, then sweetened mascarpone.

6 Just before serving, spoon sweetened mascarpone onto meringues. Top with fig slices, a piece of orange rind; spoon syrup over figs.

syrup-soaked figs Stir tea bags, rind, sugar, the water and juice in a medium saucepan over medium heat until sugar dissolves. Bring to the boil; cook 6 minutes or until syrup thickens slightly. Place figs in a large bowl. Strain syrup over figs, gently stir to combine. Reserve rind, discard tea bags. Cool.

sweetened mascarpone Beat ingredients in a medium bowl with an electric mixer until soft peaks form.

prep + cook time 1 hour (+ cooling) **serves** 8

nutritional count per serving 26.3g total fat (18.3g saturated fat); 2105kJ (503 cal); 64.5g carbohydrate; 4.4g protein; 2g fibre

tips Room temperature egg whites will beat better than cold ones. It is also a good idea when separating eggs, to do one egg at a time over a small bowl, adding to the mixer one by one; that way if you break a yolk you won't spoil the whole batch. The meringues can be made a day ahead; store in an airtight container at room temperature. Assemble just before serving.

CHOCOLATE MOUSSE CAKE WITH POMEGRANATE SYRUP

200g (6½ ounces) dark (semi-sweet) chocolate, chopped coarsely

60g (2 ounces) butter, chopped

6 eggs, separated

⅔ cup (150g) caster (superfine) sugar

CHOCOLATE MOUSSE

400g (12½ ounces) dark (semi-sweet) chocolate, chopped

¼ teaspoon ground cardamom

½ teaspoon ground cinnamon

600ml thickened (heavy) cream

POMEGRANATE SYRUP

⅓ cup (75g) caster (superfine) sugar

¼ cup (60ml) orange juice

1 medium orange (240g), rind peeled into wide strips

1 pomegranate (450g), seeds removed (see tips)

1 Preheat oven to 170°C/340°F. Grease a 22cm (9-inch) springform pan; line base and side with baking paper.

2 Place chocolate and butter in a small saucepan over low heat; stir until smooth and melted. Cool.

3 Beat egg yolks and ½ cup of the sugar in a small bowl with an electric mixer until thick and creamy. Beat in chocolate mixture. Transfer to a large bowl.

4 Beat egg whites and remaining sugar in a clean large bowl with electric mixer until soft peaks form; fold into chocolate mixture, in two batches. Spoon mixture into pan.

5 Bake cake 35 minutes or until a skewer inserted into the centre comes out with moist crumbs attached. Cool in pan.

6 Meanwhile, make chocolate mousse, then pomegranate syrup.

7 Pour mousse over cake in pan. Cover; refrigerate 6 hours or until firm. Just before serving top with pomegranate syrup.

chocolate mousse Stir chocolate in a small saucepan over low heat until smooth; stir in spices. Beat cream in a large bowl with an electric mixer until soft peaks just form. Fold in chocolate mixture until just combined.

pomegranate syrup Stir sugar, juice and rind in a small saucepan over medium heat, without boiling, until sugar dissolves. Bring to the boil. Remove pan from heat; stir in pomegranate seeds, stir to coat in syrup; cool.

prep + cook time 1 hour (+ cooling & refrigeration) **serves** 12

nutritional count per serving 39.2g total fat (23.9g saturated fat); 2481kJ (593 cal); 54.7g carbohydrate; 7.4g protein; 1.9g fibre

tips To remove seeds from a pomegranate, cut the fruit in half crossways; hold the half, cut-side down, in the palm of your hand over a bowl, then hit the outside firmly with a wooden spoon. The seeds should fall out easily; discard any white pith that falls out with them. Cake and syrup can be made a day ahead; store separately in airtight containers in the fridge.

PLUM & GINGER CROSTATA

7 large yellow-fleshed black plums
    (1.2kg), cut into thin wedges

1 egg, beaten lightly

¼ cup (55g) demerara sugar

2 tablespoons glacé ginger, chopped

PASTRY

1⅔ cups (250g) plain (all-purpose)
    flour

⅓ cup (55g) icing (confectioners')
    sugar

½ teaspoon salt

150g (4½ ounces) cold unsalted butter,
    chopped finely

¼ cup (60ml) iced water

WALNUT & GINGER PASTE

¾ cup (75g) walnuts, roasted

½ cup (115g) glacé ginger

50g (1½ ounces) soft butter

2 tablespoons instant polenta

1 tablespoon plain (all-purpose) flour

1 egg yolk

1 Make pastry.

2 Make walnut and ginger paste.

3 Preheat oven to 190°C/375°F.

4 Roll out pastry between two pieces of floured baking paper until 35cm (14-inch) round. Remove top piece of baking paper; carefully lift baking paper with pastry onto a large oven tray. Using a 26cm (10-inch) bowl or plate as a guide, mark a round in the centre of the pastry. Spread walnut and ginger paste in the marked round.

5 Starting at the edge of the filled round, place plum wedges in concentric circles. Carefully fold pastry edge in, pleating it as you go to partially cover the outside circle of plums. Brush folded edge with egg. Sprinkle sugar over plums and pastry.

6 Bake crostata for 40 minutes or until pastry is golden and filling cooked. Stand on tray for 20 minutes. Just before serving, top with glacé ginger.

pastry Process flour, icing sugar and salt until combined. Add butter; process until mixture resembles breadcrumbs. Add the water; pulse until mixture almost comes together. Turn dough onto a work surface and form into a thin disc. Wrap in plastic wrap; freeze 30 minutes only (see tip).

walnut & ginger paste Process ingredients until mixture forms a smooth paste.

prep + cook time 1 hour 15 minutes **serves** 8

nutritional count per serving 29g total fat (14.3g saturated fat); 2267kJ (542 cal); 61g carbohydrate; 7g protein; 4.3g fibre

tip If you don't plan to use the pastry after 30 minutes, place it in the refrigerator for at least 1 hour or up to a day.

serving suggestion Serve with thick (double) cream or ice-cream.

SAGE
TURNIPS
BROCCOLINI
APPLES
BLOOD ORANGES
GRAPEFRUIT
WHITE CABBAGE
WINTER
POTATOES
ROSEMARY
SILVER BEET
PEARS
SPINACH
QUINCE

VEGETABLES

The hardy winter garden abounds in leafy greens and root vegetables. Luckily the frosty months are when we crave warming bakes, stews and soups all of which would be incomplete without these vegies.

FRUIT

Winter is a time when most things hide from the cold. Not so with citrus fruits, crisp apples, pears and the quirky quince. They happily wait in the orchard — nature's cold storage — until required.

WHOLEMEAL SPAGHETTI WITH BROCCOLINI & GARLIC CRUMBS

6 slices wholemeal bread (270g),
    discard crusts

375g (12 ounces) wholemeal spaghetti

420g (13½ ounces) broccolini,
    ends trimmed

150g (4½ ounces) sugar snap peas,
    trimmed

⅓ cup (80ml) extra virgin olive oil

2 cloves garlic, crushed

1 small red chilli, seeded,
    chopped finely

2 green onions (scallions),
    chopped finely

1 medium zucchini (120g),
    sliced thinly

2 anchovy fillets, chopped finely

2 teaspoons finely grated lemon rind

¼ cup (60ml) lemon juice

75g (2½ ounces) soft goat's cheese,
    crumbled

1 Tear bread into small pieces.

2 Cook pasta in a large saucepan of boiling water until almost tender. Add broccolini and peas to water for last 5 minutes of pasta cooking time. Drain; reserve ¼ cup cooking water.

3 Meanwhile, heat half the oil in a large frying pan over medium-high heat; cook bread pieces, garlic and chilli, stirring frequently, for 5 minutes or until browned and crisp. Drain on paper towel.

4 Heat remaining oil in same cleaned pan; cook green onion, zucchini and anchovy, stirring, for 5 minutes or until zucchini is tender.

5 Combine pasta mixture and zucchini mixture in a large bowl with rind, juice and reserved cooking water.

6 Serve pasta topped with garlic crumbs and goat's cheese.

prep + cook time 40 minutes **serves** 4

nutritional count per serving 25.3g total fat (6g saturated fat); 2868kJ (685 cal); 82.2g carbohydrate; 26.2g protein; 10.9g fibre

tip You can use green beans or frozen peas instead of sugar snap peas, if you prefer.

FOR A DELICIOUS TWIST ON THIS RECIPE, SWAP BROCCOLI FOR CAULIFLOWER AND BLUE CHEESE FOR PARMESAN. FOR VEGETARIANS OMIT THE PROSCIUTTO AND ADD A TABLESPOON EACH OF SUNFLOWER SEEDS AND PEPITAS TO THE BREADCRUMB MIX.

CAULIFLOWER MAC 'N' CHEESE

750g (1½-pound) cauliflower, trimmed, cut into large florets

1½ tablespoons extra virgin olive oil

300g (9½ ounces) casserecci or other short tubular pasta

100g (3 ounces) butter, chopped

½ cup (75g) plain (all-purpose) flour

3¼ cups (810ml) hot milk

2 tablespoons wholegrain mustard

½ cup (60g) coarsely grated cheddar

¾ cup (60g) finely grated parmesan

6 slices prosciutto (90g), chopped

2 tablespoons panko (japanese) breadcrumbs

2 tablespoons fresh flat-leaf parsley

1 Preheat oven to 240°C/475°F. Grease four 2-cup (500ml) ovenproof dishes.

2 Place cauliflower on a large oven tray, drizzle with oil and season; toss well to combine. Roast 15 minutes or until almost tender and browned. Reduce oven to 200°C/400°F.

3 Meanwhile, cook pasta in a large saucepan of boiling salted water 6 minutes (or 2 minutes less than directed on the packet); drain. Return pasta to pan.

4 Meanwhile, melt butter in a medium saucepan over medium heat, add flour; cook, stirring until mixture bubbles and thickens. Gradually whisk in milk until smooth; cook, whisking, until mixture boils and thickens. Remove from heat; stir in mustard, cheddar, two-thirds of the parmesan and the prosciutto until cheeses melt. Add cheese sauce to pasta in pan; toss to combine.

5 Spoon pasta mixture into ovenproof dishes, press cauliflower pieces into pasta. Top with combined breadcrumbs and remaining parmesan.

6 Bake for 20 minutes or until crumbs are golden and mixture is heated through.

prep + cook time 45 minutes **serves** 4

nutritional count per serving 49g total fat (26.7g saturated fat); 3994kJ (954 cal); 86.5g carbohydrate; 37.8g protein; 8.3g fibre

tip Cooking the pasta in boiling water for 2 minutes less than recommended on the packet directions means that it will still be quite firm. The pasta will be perfectly cooked once it has spent time in the oven.

MOROCCAN ROAST CHICKEN & CAULIFLOWER

3 teaspoons ground cumin

3 teaspoons ground coriander

3 teaspoons sweet paprika

2 teaspoons ground turmeric

2 teaspoons ground cinnamon

1 teaspoon sea salt flakes

1 large red onion (300g),
   chopped coarsely

3 cloves garlic, halved

2 teaspoons finely grated ginger

½ cup (125ml) extra virgin olive oil

2 tablespoons water

6 chicken marylands (2kg)

1kg (2-pound) cauliflower, trimmed,
   cut into large florets

1½ tablespoons pomegranate molasses

1 large red onion (300g), extra,
   sliced thinly

3 bulbs baby fennel (390g), trimmed,
   each cut into 6 wedges

1 cup (250ml) chicken stock

280g (9 ounces) sicilian green olives,
   sliced

1 cup firmly packed fresh coriander
   (cilantro) sprigs

1 Dry-fry spices and salt in a small frying pan over medium heat, stirring, 2 minutes or until fragrant and lightly toasted. Place spice mixture in a food processor bowl with chopped onion, garlic, ginger, ⅓ cup of the oil and the water; process until mixture forms a smooth paste.

2 Using a metal skewer or fork, prick chicken all over; rub spice paste all over chicken. Place chicken in a large bowl. Cover; refrigerate 1 hour.

3 Preheat oven to 240°C/475°F.

4 Meanwhile, place cauliflower on a baking-paper-lined oven tray. Drizzle with remaining oil then pomegranate molasses; toss well to combine. Season. Spread into a single layer. Bake 18 minutes or until browned and almost tender. Set aside.

5 Reduce oven to 200°C/400°F. Place sliced onion and fennel in a large roasting pan. Place marylands and marinade, skin-side up on top, pour in stock; roast 30 minutes. Return cauliflower to oven; roast 5 minutes or until heated through and chicken is cooked through.

6 Serve chicken topped with olives and coriander and with cauliflower.

prep + cook time 1 hour 30 minutes (+ refrigeration) **serves** 4

nutritional count per serving 56.2g total fat (11g saturated fat); 3844kJ (918 cal); 22g carbohydrate; 75.4g protein; 12.8g fibre

serving suggestion Serve with Greek-style yoghurt.

YOU COULD SERVE THIS TART AS A CHEESE COURSE IN A MENU, OR MAKE A LUNCH OR BRUNCH OUT OF IT BY SERVING IT WITH A BITTER LEAF SALAD.

APPLE & BRIE TART

2 medium red apples (300g), unpeeled

1 tablespoon olive oil

300g (9½ ounces) brie

400g (12½ ounces) fresh ricotta

1 tablespoon fresh thyme leaves

1 egg

2 teaspoons wholegrain mustard

¼ cup (85g) grapefruit or lime
   marmalade, warmed

8 sprigs fresh thyme

SOUR CREAM PASTRY

1⅔ cups (250g) plain (all-purpose)
   flour

80g (2½ ounces) cold butter, chopped

½ cup (120g) sour cream

1 egg yolk

1 Make sour cream pastry.

2 Oil a 24cm (9½-inch) round loose-based tart tin. Roll pastry between sheets of lightly floured baking paper until large enough to line tin. Ease pastry into tin, press into base and side; trim edge. Freeze 15 minutes.

3 Preheat oven to 180°C/350°F.

4 Place tart on an oven tray. Line pastry case with baking paper, fill with dried beans or rice. Bake 15 minutes. Remove paper and beans; bake a further 10 minutes or until base is dry and cooked. Cool.

5 Meanwhile, using a mandoline or sharp knife, cut apples lengthways into 5mm (¼-inch) thick slices. Heat half the oil in a large frying pan over medium heat. Add half the apples; cook 30 seconds each side or until golden. Drain on paper towel. Repeat with remaining apple slices.

6 Finely chop three-quarters of the brie. Cut remaining brie into thin slices; reserve. Combine chopped brie, ricotta, thyme leaves, egg and mustard in a medium bowl; season. Spread mixture into tart shell. Arrange reserved sliced brie over cheese mixture, overlapping slices. Brush with marmalade.

7 Bake tart 30 minutes. Top tart with apple; bake a further 5 minutes or until apple is warmed through. Serve tart warm topped with thyme sprigs.

sour cream pastry Process flour and butter until crumbly. Add cream and yolk, process until mixture comes together. Knead pastry on floured surface until smooth. Wrap in plastic wrap; refrigerate 30 minutes.

prep + cook time 1 hour 45 minutes (+ refrigeration) **serves** 8

nutritional count per serving 33.5g total fat (18.1g saturated fat); 2153kJ (514 cal); 36.8g carbohydrate; 16.5g protein; 2.2g fibre

PANCETTA & SILVER BEET
FLATBREADS
(RECIPE PAGE 136)

PANCETTA & SILVER BEET FLATBREADS

1½ cups (225g) plain (all-purpose) flour

½ cup (75g) self-raising flour

¼ cup (70g) Greek-style yoghurt

¾ cup (180ml) water

2 tablespoons olive oil

200g (6½ ounces) sliced pancetta

375g (12 ounces) silver beet (swiss chard), trimmed, shredded thickly

1 clove garlic, sliced

2 teaspoons grated lemon rind

150g (4½ ounces) mozzarella, sliced thinly

2 teaspoons olive oil, extra

1 Sift flours into a large bowl; stir in yoghurt and the water until combined. Turn dough onto a floured surface; knead 2 minutes. Place dough in bowl, cover with plastic wrap; stand in a warm place 30 minutes.

2 Heat half the oil in a large frying pan over high heat; cook pancetta, turning, until browned and crisp. Drain on paper towel.

3 Cook silver beet, garlic and rind in same pan, stirring, until silver beet is just wilted.

4 Preheat an oiled barbecue (or chargrill plate) to medium-high. Divide dough into four pieces. Roll each piece on a floured surface into 15cm x 30cm (6-inch x 12-inch) ovals. Brush dough with remaining oil. Cook dough on heated oiled barbecue for 2 minutes or until golden underneath. Turn flatbreads, top with silver beet mixture, mozzarella and pancetta; cook until cheese melts.

5 Serve flatbreads drizzled with extra oil.

prep + cook time 40 minutes (+ standing) **serves** 4
nutritional count per serving 29.5g total fat (11g saturated fat); 2685kJ (641 cal); 58.1g carbohydrate; 33.4g protein; 4g fibre

(photograph page 135)

GAI LAN WITH OYSTER SAUCE

½ cup (125ml) peanut oil

8 cloves garlic, sliced thinly

1kg (2 pounds) gai lan, trimmed, halved

1½ tablespoons peanut oil

¼ cup (60ml) oyster sauce

2 tablespoons light soy sauce

1 fresh long red chilli, sliced thinly

1 Place oil and sliced garlic in a wok over medium heat. Once oil starts to sizzle, stir garlic continously, 2 minutes or until golden. Remove garlic immediately with a slotted spoon; drain on paper towel. Remove wok from heat; reserve 1½ tablespoons oil from the wok, discard remaining.

2 Cook gai lan stems in a large saucepan of boiling water for 1 minute. Add gai lan leaves; cook a further 30 seconds or until leaves and stems are almost tender. Drain well.

3 Heat reserved oil in wok over high heat, add gai lan and sauces; stir-fry 2 minutes or until mixture is heated through. Serve topped with fried garlic and chilli.

prep + cook time 10 minutes **serves** 6 (as a side)
nutritional count per serving 6.6g total fat (1.2g saturated fat); 438kJ (105 cal); 5.2g carbohydrate; 3.7g protein; 4.1g fibre
tip Left over garlic frying oil can be saved and used for future stir-fries, or used for roasting vegetables.

GAI LAN WITH OYSTER SAUCE

VEAL SCHNITZEL WITH WINTER SLAW

1¼ cups (95g) panko (japanese)
   breadcrumbs

¼ cup (20g) finely grated parmesan

2 tablespoons finely chopped
   fresh flat-leaf parsley

1 tablespoon finely grated lemon rind

8 veal schnitzels (800g)

¼ cup (35g) plain (all-purpose) flour

2 eggs, beaten lightly

olive oil, for shallow-frying

2 medium lemons (140g),
   cut into wedges

WINTER SLAW

500g (1 pound) brussels sprouts

1 medium fennel (300g)

1 stalk celery (150g), trimmed

½ small red onion (50g)

1 cup loosely packed young
   celery leaves

1 tablespoon baby capers

½ cup (40g) finely grated parmesan

¼ cup (60ml) lemon juice

2 teaspoons dijon mustard

1 tablespoon honey

¼ cup (60ml) extra virgin olive oil

1 Combine breadcrumbs, parmesan, parsley and rind in a shallow bowl. Coat veal in flour; shake off excess. Dip veal in egg, then coat in breadcrumb mixture. Refrigerate until required.

2 Make winter slaw.

3 Heat oil in a large frying pan over medium-high heat; cook veal 2 minutes each side or until golden and cooked through.

4 Serve veal with winter slaw and lemon wedges.

winter slaw Trim and separate leaves from sprouts. Add leaves to a large saucepan of boiling salted water until bright green; drain. Add leaves to a bowl of iced water until cold; drain well. Using a mandoline or V-slicer, thinly slice fennel, celery and onion. Place fennel, celery and onion in a large bowl with sprouts, celery leaves, capers and parmesan; toss gently to combine. Whisk juice, mustard and honey in a small bowl until combined. Gradually add oil, whisking continuously until combined. Season to taste. Just before serving, add dressing to slaw; toss gently to combine.

prep + cook time 45 minutes serves 4

nutritional count per serving 44.5g total fat (11g saturated fat); 4079kJ (975 cal); 36.2g carbohydrate; 101.9g protein; 10.6g fibre

tips The veal can be crumbed 6 hours ahead. Keep covered in the refrigerator. The slaw can be prepared 6 hours ahead; add the dressing just before serving. Sprinkle the slaw with a few fennel fronds, if you like.

There's something serene about a winter morning on the river. Wisps of mist hover over the water and the fishing lines gently bob in anticipation of a bite. Row back to the river bank to cook up your catch.

ROAST VEAL RACK WITH CELERIAC & POTATO GRATIN

2kg (4-pound) veal rack (8 cutlets)

1 cup (250ml) water

¼ cup (70g) dijon mustard

2 tablespoons horseradish cream

2 cloves garlic, crushed

1½ tablespoons plain (all-purpose) flour

2 teaspoons wholegrain mustard

2 cups (500ml) beef stock

2 tablespoons finely chopped tarragon

1 tablespoon coarsely chopped fresh thyme

¼ cup finely chopped fresh flat-leaf parsley

CELERIAC & POTATO GRATIN

600ml thickened (heavy) cream

3 cloves garlic, sliced thinly

3 teaspoons coarsely chopped fresh thyme leaves

1 medium celeriac (celery root) (750g), trimmed

3 medium potatoes (600g)

50g (1½ ounces) smoked cheddar, grated coarsely

3 sprigs thyme, extra

1 Preheat oven to 180°C/350°F.

2 Make celeriac and potato gratin.

3 Meanwhile, place veal on a wire rack in a flameproof roasting pan; pour the water into the base of the pan. Combine dijon mustard, horseradish and garlic in a small bowl. Spread mustard mixture over veal; season. Roast veal for last 45 minutes of gratin cooking time or until cooked as desired. Transfer veal to a plate, cover; rest for 10 minutes.

4 Heat the roasting pan over medium-high heat, add flour; cook, whisking, until mixture is smooth and bubbly. Add wholegrain mustard and stock; stir until mixture boils and thickens. Season to taste.

5 Combine herbs; press onto veal. Cut veal into cutlets; serve with gratin and mustard sauce.

celeriac & potato gratin Place cream, garlic and thyme in a medium saucepan over medium heat; bring to a simmer. Remove from heat; stand 10 minutes. Meanwhile, using a mandoline or V-slicer, thinly slice celeriac and potatoes; combine in a large bowl. Layer celeriac and potato with cream mixture and salt and pepper in a 1.5-litre (6-cup) round ovenproof dish. Sprinkle with cheddar. Cover with foil; bake 1 hour. Uncover, bake 20 minutes or until tender and golden. Top with thyme sprigs.

prep + cook time 1 hour 50 minutes **serves** 8

nutritional count per serving 34.6g total fat (20.8g saturated fat); 2530kJ (604 cal); 17.4g carbohydrate; 52.9g protein; 6.4g fibre

serving suggestion Serve with green beans.

BEEF & MOZZARELLA MEATBALLS WITH FENNEL & SILVER BEET

1kg (2 pounds) minced (ground) beef (see tips)

1 cup (70g) stale breadcrumbs

1 tablespoon finely grated lemon rind

1 cup (80g) finely grated parmesan

2 eggs

1 cup finely chopped fresh flat-leaf parsley

4 cloves garlic, crushed

80g (2½ ounces) mozzarella, cut into 1cm (½-inch) pieces

⅓ cup (80ml) olive oil

2 medium brown onions (300g), chopped finely

1 medium fennel bulb (300g), trimmed, sliced thinly

3½ cups (980g) bottled tomato passata

1 cup (250ml) chicken or beef stock

3 large silver beet (swiss chard) leaves (130g), trimmed, shredded finely

500g (1 pound) cavatelli or other short chunky pasta

2 tablespoons finely grated parmesan, extra

¼ cup fresh flat-leaf parsley leaves, extra

1 Combine beef, breadcrumbs, rind, parmesan, eggs, chopped parsley and half the garlic in a large bowl; season. Roll rounded tablespoons of mixture into balls, press a piece of mozzarella into the centre of each meatball, shaping as you go to completely enclose the cheese. Place meatballs on a tray, cover; refrigerate 20 minutes.

2 Preheat oven to 180°C/350°F.

3 Heat 2 tablespoons of the oil in a large frying pan over high heat. Add half the meatballs; cook 5 minutes or until browned all over, shaking pan occasionally. Transfer meatballs to a 3-litre (12-cup) ovenproof dish. Repeat with 1 tablespoon of oil and remaining meatballs.

4 Wipe out pan. Heat remaining oil in same pan over high heat; cook onion, fennel and remaining garlic, stirring, 5 minutes or until softened. Add fennel mixture to meatballs with passata, stock and silver beet; stir until combined. Season.

5 Bake, covered, 45 minutes or until fennel is tender.

6 Meanwhile, 15 mintues before meatballs are ready, cook pasta in a large saucepan of boiling salted water until almost tender; drain and keep warm.

7 Serve pasta topped with meatballs, extra parmesan and extra parsley.

prep + cook time 4 hours (+ refrigeration) **serves** 6

nutritional count per serving 35.3g total fat (11.1g saturated fat); 3840kJ (917 cal); 80.1g carbohydrate; 64.2g protein; 10.8g fibre

tips It is best to use a mince that isn't too lean otherwise the meatballs will be dry. This recipe is suitable to freeze at the end of step 4. Cavatelli pasta resembles a split hot dog bun in shape. It is available from some delis and green grocers. You can use any other short or tubular pasta instead.

BE EXTREMELY CAREFUL WHEN BLENDING HOT SOUP – LET IT COOL A LITTLE FIRST. DON'T OVER-FILL THE BLENDER, ONE-THIRD TO HALF-FULL IS A GOOD GUIDE, AND MAKE SURE THE LID IS SECURE. ALTERNATIVELY, USE A STICK BLENDER.

PARSNIP SOUP WITH KALE CHIPS

2kg (4 pounds) parsnips, peeled, chopped coarsely

2 medium brown onions (300g), chopped coarsely

1 stalk celery (150g), trimmed

3 cloves garlic, quartered

1.5 litres (6 cups) water

1 litre (4 cups) chicken or vegetable stock

⅓ cup (80ml) olive oil

6 cloves garlic, bruised, extra

½ cup (125ml) pouring cream

2 tablespoons lemon juice

KALE CHIPS

200g (6½ ounces) green kale, washed, dried

1 clove garlic, crushed

2 tablespoons extra virgin olive oil

2 tablespoons dukkah

1 Place parsnip, onion, celery, quartered garlic, the water and stock in a large saucepan; bring to the boil. Reduce heat; simmer, covered, 1 hour or until tender. Remove pan from heat; cool, uncovered, 10 minutes.

2 Meanwhile, heat oil with extra garlic in a small saucepan over medium heat. When oil begins to sizzle; remove pan from heat. Cool. When cool, discard garlic.

3 Meanwhile, make kale chips.

4 Blend or process soup, in batches, until smooth. Return soup to pan; stir in cream, over medium-high heat, until hot. Season. Stir in juice.

5 Serve soup drizzled with garlic oil and topped with kale chips.

kale chips Preheat oven to 220°C/425°F. Tear the leafy part of the kale from stalks then tear into 3cm (1½-inch) pieces. Discard stalks. Place kale on two large oven trays lined with baking paper. Combine garlic and oil; drizzle half over each tray of kale, then toss well to combine. Spread kale out in single layer. Bake 8 minutes, turning kale and swapping trays from top to bottom, halfway through cooking time, or until kale is crisp. Season with salt; sprinkle with dukkah.

prep + cook time 1 hour 20 minutes (+ standing) **serves** 8

nutritional count per serving 21.3g total fat (6g saturated fat); 1496kJ (357 cal); 29.6g carbohydrate; 6.9g protein; 10.7g fibre

tip This soup is suitable to freeze.

IF YOU USE A POTATO RICER TO MASH POTATOES, ADD PRESSED POTATOES TO THE WARM CREAM, THEN STIR THE BUTTER AND PARMESAN IN. NEVER ATTEMPT TO MASH POTATOES IN A FOOD PROCESSOR AS IT WILL MAKE THE TEXTURE GLUEY.

BEEF & PORCINI MUSHROOM STEW WITH PARMESAN MASH

25g (¾ ounce) dried porcini mushrooms

1 cup (250ml) beef stock

2 tablespoons olive oil

1.5kg (3 pounds) gravy beef, cut into 5cm (2-inch) pieces

1 large brown onion (200g), chopped coarsely

2 cloves garlic, crushed

2 tablespoons tomato paste

400g (12½ ounces) canned cherry tomatoes

1 bay leaf

250g (4 ounces) button mushrooms, halved

2 tablespoons coarsely chopped fresh flat-leaf parsley

PARMESAN MASH

1kg (2 pounds) floury potatoes (see tip), peeled, cut into large pieces

¾ cup (180ml) pouring cream

75g (2½ ounces) butter, chopped

1 cup (80g) finely grated parmesan

1 Place porcini mushrooms and stock in a small bowl; soak for 10 minutes. Drain, reserving stock. Finely chop mushrooms.

2 Heat oil in a large casserole or heavy-based saucepan over medium-high heat; cook beef, in batches, turning until browned all over. Remove from dish.

3 Cook onion and garlic in same dish, stirring, until softened. Return beef to dish with paste, tomatoes, bay leaf, porcini mushrooms and reserved stock; bring to the boil. Reduce heat to a simmer; cook, covered, 30 minutes. Add button mushrooms; cook, uncovered, a further 1 hour or until meat is tender. Season to taste.

4 Meanwhile, make parmesan mash.

5 Serve beef stew with parmesan mash, sprinkled with parsley.

parmesan mash Boil potatoes in a saucepan of salted water until tender. Drain; leave for a few minutes to dry. Heat cream and butter in same pan over medium-low heat; add potatoes, mashing into milk mixture with a potato masher until smooth. Remove from heat; stir in parmesan until combined. Season to taste.

prep + cook time 1 hour 40 minutes **serves** 4

nutritional count per serving 97.5g total fat (44.9g saturated fat); 5944kJ (1420 cal); 40.6g carbohydrate; 91.9g protein; 9.5g fibre

tip Floury potatoes have a high starch content so tend to fall apart when cooked. They are great for roasting, as their flesh becomes fluffy and the outside crisp, and for mashing, as they will be very creamy. Varieties include king edward and coliban.

TROUT WITH LEMON &
THYME BUTTER
(RECIPE PAGE 154)

TROUT WITH LEMON & THYME BUTTER

4 x 300g (9½ ounces) rainbow trout, cleaned

640g (1¼ pounds) baby leeks, trimmed, washed

2 tablespoons olive oil

2 medium lemons (140g), halved

12 fresh sprigs thyme

LEMON & THYME BUTTER

175g (5½ ounces) lightly salted butter, softened

2 cloves garlic, crushed

2 tablespoons fresh finely chopped thyme

1 tablespoon lemon juice

1 Make lemon and thyme butter.

2 Pat fish dry with paper towel; season both sides liberally.

3 Cook leeks in a saucepan of boiling salted water 2 minutes or until just tender; drain.

4 Heat half the oil in a large frying pan over high heat, add one-third of the lemon and thyme butter; swirl pan to coat base wtih butter. Once butter starts to foam, add 2 fish, 2 lemon halves, cut-side down, and 6 sprigs thyme. Cook 7 minutes each side or until fish is just cooked through. Transfer to an oven tray; cover loosely with foil. Repeat with remaining oil, another one-third butter, trout, lemon halves and thyme sprigs.

5 Heat remaining butter in same pan; cook leeks 2 minutes or until golden. Divide ingredients among plates; spoon over pan juices to serve.

lemon & thyme butter Stir ingredients together in a small bowl; season to taste.

prep + cook time 25 minutes **serves** 4

nutritional count per serving 60.7g total fat (29.2g saturated fat); 3022kJ (722 cal); 4.9g carbohydrate; 39.1g protein; 3.8g fibre

serving suggestion Serve the trout in soft buns with mixed salad greens.

(photograph page 153)

ROAST PORK WITH APPLE SAUCE

The rind of the pork will crackle better if you leave it unwrapped in the fridge overnight.

6-point rack of pork (1.6kg), rind scored

1 tablespoon olive oil

1 tablespoon coarse cooking (kosher) salt

2 teaspoons fennel seeds, crushed

APPLE SAUCE

3 large granny smith apples (600g), peeled, cored, sliced thickly

½ cup (125ml) water

1 teaspoon caster (superfine) sugar

¼ teaspoon ground cinnamon

1 Preheat oven to 250°C/480°F.

2 Pat the pork dry with paper towel. Place the pork on a rack in a roasting pan. Rub the rind with the oil, then the combined salt and crushed fennel seeds.

3 Roast pork 40 minutes or until the skin blisters. Reduce oven to 180°C/350°F; roast a further 35 minutes or until pork is just cooked. To test if pork is cooked, insert a meat thermometer into a middle section of the meat; it should register 62°C/145°F. Alternatively, insert a metal skewer; the juices should run clear.

4 Meanwhile, make apple sauce.

5 Serve pork with apple sauce.

apple sauce Place apples and the water in a medium saucepan; simmer, uncovered, 15 minutes or until apple is soft. Stir in sugar and cinnamon.

prep + cook time 1 hour 25 minutes **serves** 6

nutritional count per serving 17.2g total fat (6.1g saturated fat); 1372kJ (328 cal); 7.3g carbohydrate; 35.7g protein; 1.2g fibre

tip Crush the fennel seeds in a mortar and pestle if you have one, otherwise you can chop them with a knife.

serving suggestion Serve with seasonal vegetables such as roast potatoes, brussels sprouts or celeriac.

ROAST PORK WITH
APPLE SAUCE

SAGE IS A PERENNIAL WINTER HERB CHARACTERISED BY A PUNGENT CAMPHOR-LIKE TASTE WHEN RAW. FRYING IN BUTTER OR OIL MORPHS BOTH THE TASTE AND TEXTURE, TRANSFORMING THE LEAVES INTO CRISP MOREISH BITES WITH A SWEETISH EDGE.

SAGE & OLIVE SAUTEED POTATOES

500g (1 pound) baby new potatoes, halved

1kg (2 pounds) kipfler (fingerling) potatoes, scrubbed, halved lengthways

⅔ cup (160ml) extra virgin olive oil

1 bulb garlic, halved crossways

½ cup fresh sage leaves

½ cup (80g) kalamata olives, halved, pitted

2 medium lemons (280g), rind peeled in wide strips

1 Preheat oven to 160°C/325°F.

2 Place baby potatoes in a large saucepan with enough water to cover. Bring to the boil; boil 5 minutes (the potatoes will be sligthly undercooked). Remove potatoes with a slotted spoon; drain. Place potatoes, cut-side up, on a clean tea towel to dry.

3 Cook kipfler potatoes in same water, return water to the boil; boil 5 minutes (the potatoes will be slightly undercooked). Drain. Place potatoes, cut-side up, on the tea towel to dry.

4 Meanwhile, heat oil with garlic in a small saucepan over the lowest heat for 20 minutes. Increase heat to medium. Add sage, in two batches, for 30 seconds or until crisp. Remove with a slotted spoon; drain on paper towel. Remove garlic from oil; reserve. Turn off the heat under oil.

5 Heat 2 tablespoons of garlic-sage oil in a large frying pan; cook one-third of the potatoes, cut-side down first, for 2 minutes, turn and cook a further minute or until deep golden. Transfer to a roasting pan; keep warm in the oven. Repeat cooking with another 2 tablespoons of oil and a third of potatoes; add to the roasting pan. Repeat cooking with 1 tablespoon of oil, remaining potatoes, olives and lemon strips.

6 Add potatoes, olives, lemon strips and reserved garlic to the roasting pan, season to taste; toss to combine. Serve topped with sage.

prep + cook time 1 hour serves 8

nutritional count per serving 14.9g total fat (2.3g saturated fat); 1099kJ (263 cal); 24.1g carbohydrate; 5g protein; 4.7g fibre

tip Remaining garlic-infused oil can be used in salad dressings.

LEAFY GREENS THRIVE IN THE COOLNESS OF A SOUTHERN HEMISPHERE WINTER AND ARE AT THEIR ABUNDANT BEST. THE SPINACH CAN BE REPLACED WITH SILVER BEET OR EVEN KALE IF YOU PREFER, SIMPLY DISCARD THE TOUGH CENTRE STALKS FIRST.

LAMB, SPINACH & FETTA PIE

¼ cup (60ml) olive oil

2 medium onions (300g), chopped finely

3 trimmed celery stalks (450g), chopped finely

4 cloves garlic, crushed

1kg (2 pounds) minced (ground) lamb

½ cup (125ml) dry red wine

1½ cup (375ml) vegetable stock

800g (1½ pounds) canned crushed tomatoes

⅓ cup (95g) tomato paste

1 tablespoon fresh chopped oregano

2 cinnamon sticks

150g (4½ ounces) greek fetta, crumbled

500g (1 pound) baby spinach leaves

2 sheets shortcrust pastry

1 egg

1 egg yolk

1 teaspoon sea salt flakes

1 teaspoon fennel seeds

1 Preheat oven to 220°C/425°F.

2 Heat oil in a large frying pan over medium heat; cook onion and celery, stirring, for 5 minutes or until browned lightly. Add garlic; cook 1 minute.

3 Increase heat to high, add lamb; cook, stirring, until browned, breaking it up with the back of a spoon. Add wine; simmer 2 minutes. Add stock, tomatoes, paste, oregano and cinnamon; simmer, uncovered, 35 minutes or until the liquid has evaporated and sauce is thick. Remove from heat. Cool.

4 Stir fetta and spinach into lamb mixture; season to taste. Spoon lamb mixture into a 20cm (8-inch) round pie tin or 1.5-litre (6-cup) ovenproof dish.

5 Using a fluted pastry wheel, or a knife, cut each sheet of pastry into nine equal rectangles. Place pastry rectangles, slightly overlapping to cover filling in two concentric circles then cut a slit in the top of the pie. Brush pastry with combined beaten egg and egg yolk; sprinkle with salt and fennel seeds.

6 Bake pie 25 minutes or until pastry is a deep golden; cover the pastry with pieces of foil if it starts to overbrown. Stand 10 minutes before serving.

prep + cook time 1 hour 20 minutes (+ standing) **serves** 6

nutritional count per serving 52.7g total fat (20.2g saturated fat); 3421kJ (817 cal); 31.4g carbohydrate; 49.6g protein; 6.3g fibre

MANDARIN ALMOND CAKES WITH CANDIED CUMQUATS

....

1¼ cups (185g) self-raising flour

½ teaspoon bicarbonate of soda
(baking soda)

1 cup (120g) ground almonds

1¼ cups (275g) caster (superfine)
sugar

½ cup (125ml) extra virgin olive oil

1 tablespoon finely grated
mandarin rind

½ cup (125ml) strained freshly
squeezed mandarin juice

3 eggs, beaten lightly

1¼ cups (290g) fresh ricotta

½ cup (80g) icing (confectioners')
sugar

⅔ cup (160ml) thick (double) cream
(51% fat)

CANDIED CUMQUATS

325g (10½ ounces) cumquats, halved,
seeds removed

1 cup (220g) caster (superfine) sugar

¾ cup (180ml) water

2 tablespoons lime juice

1 Make candied cumquats

2 Preheat oven to 180°C/350°F. Grease eight 10cm (4-inch) springform pans.
Line bases and sides with baking paper.

3 Sift flour, soda and ground almonds into a large bowl, pushing mixture through
with a wooden spoon. Stir in caster sugar. Whisk oil, rind, juice and eggs in a small
bowl; add to dry ingredients, whisk until mixture is smooth. Spoon mixture into pans.

4 Bake cakes 25 minutes or until a skewer inserted into the centre comes out clean.
Stand in tins until cooled.

5 Meanwhile, process ricotta and sifted icing sugar until smooth; transfer to a
medium bowl. Gently fold in cream until combined.

6 Serve cakes topped with ricotta cream and candied cumquats.

candied cumquats Place cumquats in a small saucepan of water; bring to the boil.
Drain. Repeat process (this is to help remove any bitterness and soften the rind).
Stir sugar and the water in a small saucepan over low heat until sugar dissolves.
Increase heat to high; bring to the boil. Add cumquats; simmer for 30 minutes or
until soft and translucent, and syrup is reduced. Cool. Stir in juice.

prep + cook time 1 hour (+ cooling) **makes** 8

nutritional count per cake 37.8g total fat (11.7g saturated fat); 3216kJ (768 cal);
98.5g carbohydrate; 12.3g protein; 5g fibre

SPICED WALNUT & CHOCOLATE CAKE WITH POACHED QUINCE

450g (14½ ounces) walnuts, roasted lightly

75g (2½ ounces) dark (semi-sweet) chocolate, grated coarsely

1½ cups (105g) fresh fine white breadcrumbs

2 teaspoons baking powder

1½ teaspoons ground cinnamon

¼ teaspoon ground cloves

6 eggs, separated

1 cup (220g) caster (superfine) sugar

185g (6 ounces) butter, melted

500g (1 pound) mascarpone

POACHED QUINCE

5 medium quinces (1.75kg)

4½ cups (990g) caster (superfine) sugar

3 cups (750ml) water

2 cups (500ml) rosé wine

2 vanilla beans, split lengthways

1 Make poached quince.

2 Meanwhile, preheat oven to 180°C/350°F. Grease a 24cm x 34cm (9½-inches x 13½-inches) shallow rectangular cake pan; line base and sides with baking paper.

3 Pulse nuts in a food processor until finely chopped. Combine nuts, chocolate, breadcrumbs, baking powder and ground spices in a large bowl.

4 Beat yolks and sugar in a large bowl with an electric mixer until creamy. Add nut mixture; mix well. Fold in butter. Beat egg whites in a large clean bowl with an electric mixer until soft peaks form. Fold whites, in two batches, into nut mixture; pour mixture into pan.

5 Bake cake 25 minutes, rotating pan halfway through cooking time, or until a skewer inserted in the centre comes out clean. Stand cake 10 minutes, before transferring to a wire rack to cool completely in the pan.

6 Strain poached quince through a fine sieve over a bowl. Remove core from quince; cut each quarter in half lengthways. Place quince wedges on a tray, cover; refrigerate until needed. Discard peelings and vanilla. Boil 2 cups strained syrup in a medium saucepan over medium heat 15 minutes or until thickened. Cool.

7 Beat mascarpone and ½ cup reduced syrup in a small bowl with an electric mixer until almost firm peaks form.

8 Spread top of cake with mascarpone mixture; drizzle with 2 tablespoons of the remaining reduced syrup. Serve cake cut into squares with quince.

poached quince Peel quince, reserve half the peel. Quarter quince, do not core. Combine sugar, the water, wine and vanilla in a large cast iron casserole or saucepan with tight-fitting lid; stir over medium heat until sugar dissolves. Add quince and reserved peel, bring to the boil; cover with a sheet of baking paper then cover tightly with foil, or a lid. (Make sure quince is submerged in the liquid, you may need to put a plate on top of quince). Reduce heat to a gentle simmer; cook 3¼ hours or until tender and a deep red colour. Cool quince in syrup.

prep + cook time 3 hours 45 minutes (+ cooling) **serves** 8

nutritional count per serving 91g total fat (35.9g saturated fat); 4870kJ (1163 cal); 69.7g carbohydrate; 18.7g protein; 7.7g fibre

tips Depending on the variety of quince used, some will turn more of a rusty red colour while others a deep crimson. Also, cooking time can vary between types, with some needing a little longer cooking to achieve a red hue. Cake can be made up to 2 months ahead and frozen.

Australia's geography means we are lucky to have two seasons for strawberries. During summer they hail principally from Victoria, while winter strawberries are grown in Queensland.

APPLE, STRAWBERRY & ROSEMARY CRUMBLE

8 medium red apples (1.2kg)

¼ cup (55g) caster sugar

¼ cup (60ml) water

500g (1 pound) small strawberries, halved if large

1 teaspoon ground cinnamon

1 teaspoon plain (all-purpose) flour

2 teaspoons vanilla extract

⅓ cup (80ml) maple syrup

1½ cups (240g) almond kernels

1 cup (150g) self-raising flour

2 teaspoons fresh rosemary leaves, chopped finely

125g (4 ounces) cold butter, chopped finely

½ cup (110g) firmly packed brown sugar

2 tablespoons maple syrup, extra

125g (4 ounces) strawberries, halved, extra

1 Preheat oven to 180°C/350°F.

2 Peel, core and cut apples into 2cm (¾-inch) pieces. Place apple, caster sugar and the water in a large saucepan; bring to the boil, stirring to dissolve sugar. Cook, covered, over low heat, for 10 minutes or until apples are just tender.

3 Combine apples and the cooking liquid in a large bowl with strawberries, cinnamon, plain flour, extract and maple syrup. Spoon mixture into a 2-litre (8-cup) shallow ovenproof dish.

4 To make crumble, process nuts, self-raising flour and rosemary until nuts are coarsely chopped. Add butter and brown sugar; pulse until butter is almost finely chopped. Tip mixture into a large bowl. Drizzle extra maple syrup over dry ingredients, then using fingertips, rub into flour mixture until mixture begins to clump. Scatter crumble over fruit (pile crumble high on top of the fruit as it will sink down as it cooks).

5 Bake crumble for 40 minutes or until topping is golden and fruit is soft. Serve crumble topped with extra strawberries.

prep + cook time 1 hour **serves** 6

nutritional count per serving 39.6g total fat (12.6g saturated fat); 3201kJ (765 cal); 87.9g carbohydrate; 13g protein; 9.7g fibre

tip We used gala apples in this recipe. You could also use pink ladies or golden delicious apples instead.

serving suggestion Serve with thick (double) cream or ice-cream.

CHOCOLATE PEAR CAKES
(RECIPE PAGE 168)

CHOCOLATE PEAR CAKES

125g (4 ounces) unsalted butter

½ cup (110g) firmly packed light brown sugar

2 eggs

1 cup (150g) self-raising flour

2 tablespoons cocoa powder

½ teaspoon baking powder

1 tablespoon water

RASPBERRY POACHED PEARS

6 small corella pears (810g)

1 vanilla bean

1½ cup (330g) caster (superfine) sugar

3 cups (750ml) water

175g (5½ ounces) raspberries

1 Make raspberry poached pears.

2 Preheat oven to 180°C/350°F. Grease six ¾-cup (180ml) square or round pie tins; line base and sides with baking paper.

3 Beat butter and sugar in a small bowl with an electric mixer until light and fluffy. Beat in eggs, one at a time. Stir in sifted dry ingredients and the water. Spoon mixture into tins; stand two pear halves upright in each tin.

4 Bake cakes 25 minutes or until firm to the touch. Serve cakes drizzled with reserved syrup and raspberries.

raspberry poached pears Peel pears. Split vanilla bean lengthways; scrape seeds into a large saucepan. Add vanilla bean, sugar and the water; cook, stirring, over low heat until sugar dissolves. Add pears; bring to the boil. Reduce heat; simmer, uncovered, 10 minutes, turning halfway through cooking, or until pears are tender. Remove from heat, add two-thirds of the raspberries; stand 30 minutes. Using a slotted spoon, remove pears from syrup; cut in half lengthways. Bring syrup to the boil; boil 20 minutes or until thick and syrupy; add remaining raspberries.

prep + cook time 1 hour 20 minutes (+ standing) **makes** 6
nutritional count per cake 19.4g total fat (8.2g saturated fat); 2284kJ (546 cal); 86.6g carbohydrate; 6g protein; 6.2g fibre

(photograph page 167)

MAPLE BAKED WINTER FRUITS

1 medium orange (240g)

1 cup (250ml) dry white wine

3 small red apples (400g)

3 corella pears (405g)

30g (1 ounce) unsalted butter, softened

½ cup (125ml) pure maple syrup

450g (14½ ounces) rhubarb, trimmed,
    cut into 12cm (4¾-inches) lengths

250g (8 ounces) mascarpone or crème fraîche

1 Preheat oven to 180°C/350°F.

2 Using a vegetable peeler, peel rind from orange in one long strip, if possible. Squeeze juice from orange. Place juice, rind and wine in a large shallow baking dish.

3 Halve apples crossways; trim the bases slightly to give them a flat surface to sit on. Halve the pears lengthways; trim the rounded skin sides slightly, to give them a flat surface to sit on. Place apples and pears in baking dish, trimmed-side down.

4 Rub softened butter generously over apples and pears; drizzle with maple syrup. Cover dish with foil; bake 20 minutes. Add rhubarb; bake, covered, a further 10 minutes. Remove foil; bake a further 5 minutes or until all fruit is tender.

5 Combine mascarpone with 2 tablespoons of the cooking liquid from the baked fruit.

6 Serve baked fruit with mascarpone.

prep + cook time 45 minutes **serves** 6
nutritional count per serving 22g total fat (14.1g saturated fat); 1584kJ (378 cal); 39g carbohydrate; 7g protein; 7.1g fibre
serving suggestion Serve with almond biscuit or shortbread.

MAPLE BAKED
WINTER FRUITS

THE BEST PEAR VARIETIES FOR BAKING ARE WILLIAMS AND BEURRE BOSC, AS BOTH HOLD THEIR SHAPE DURING COOKING. WILLIAMS PEARS ARRIVE IN AUTUMN, WHILE BUERRE BOSC PEARS ARE IN SEASON FROM MID-AUTUMN, THROUGH WINTER TO EARLY SPRING.

PEAR & GINGER UPSIDE-DOWN CAKE

3 medium pears (630g)

1½ cups (330g) firmly packed
   brown sugar

1 cup (250ml) vegetable oil

1 medium orange (240g),
   rind finely grated

2 teaspoons finely grated fresh ginger

3 eggs

2½ cups (375g) plain (all-purpose)
   flour

2½ teaspoons baking powder

½ cup (125ml) milk

ORANGE CINNAMON SYRUP

⅓ cup (80ml) freshly squeezed
   strained orange juice

60g (2 ounces) butter

1 cup (220g) firmly packed
   brown sugar

½ teaspoon ground cinnamon

1 Preheat oven to 220°C/425°F. Grease and line a 24cm (9½-inch) round cake pan.

2 Make orange cinnamon syrup.

3 Peel and core pears; cut each into eight wedges. Arrange pear in a decorative pattern on base of cake pan; pour syrup over pears.

4 Beat sugar, oil, rind, ginger and eggs in a large bowl with an electric mixer until combined. Gently add combined sifted flour and baking powder, then milk. Carefully pour batter over pears.

5 Bake cake 10 minutes. Reduce heat to 180°C/350°F; bake a further 55 minutes or until a skewer inserted into the centre of the cake comes out clean. Cool cake completely in the pan before carefully turning out onto a platter.

orange cinnamon syrup Place ingredients in a small saucepan; bring to the boil. Reduce heat; simmer over medium heat 3 minutes or until thickened slightly. Cool.

prep + cook time 1 hour 20 minutes **serves** 8

nutritional count per serving 37.8g total fat (7.2g saturated fat); 3382kJ (808 cal); 110g carbohydrate; 8.5g protein; 4.1g fibre

serving suggestion Serve with vanilla ice-cream.

TANGELOS ARE A CROSS BETWEEN A TANGERINE AND A GRAPEFRUIT. THEY LOOK LIKE AN ESPECIALLY RICHLY COLOURED, SMALLISH ORANGE WITH A SLIGHT NECK AT THE STEM END, AND TASTE LIKE A SWEET ORANGE. THEIR THICK SKIN PEELS EASILY AND THEY ARE EASY TO SEPARATE INTO SEGMENTS.

TANGELO TART WITH CANDIED BLOOD ORANGES

1½ cups (225g) plain (all-purpose) flour

2 tablespoons icing (confectioners') sugar

125g (4 ounces) cold butter, chopped coarsely

1 egg yolk

1 tablespoon chilled water

1 tablespoon finely grated tangelo rind

½ cup (125ml) strained freshly squeezed tangelo juice

5 eggs

¾ cup (165g) caster (superfine) sugar

1¼ cups (310ml) pouring cream

1 tablespoon icing (confectioners') sugar, extra

CANDIED BLOOD ORANGES

½ cup (110g) caster (superfine) sugar

1½ cups (375ml) water

½ cup (125ml) strained freshly squeezed blood orange juice

3 medium blood oranges (480g), cut into 5mm (¼-inch) slices

½ cup (180g) honey

1 Process flour, sugar and butter until mixture resembles breadcrumbs. Add egg yolk and the water; process until ingredients just come together. Wrap pastry in plastic wrap; refrigerate 30 minutes.

2 Grease a 3cm (1¼-inch) deep, 23cm (9¼-inch) round loose-based tart tin. Roll pastry between sheets of baking paper until 3mm (⅛-inch) thick and large enough to line the tin. Lift pastry into tin, ease into base and side, trim edge; prick base all over with a fork. Cover; refrigerate 20 minutes.

3 Meanwhile, preheat oven to 190°C/375°F.

4 Place tin on an oven tray; line pastry with baking paper, fill with dried beans or rice. Bake 10 minutes. Remove paper and beans; bake a further 10 minutes or until browned lightly. Cool on tray.

5 Reduce oven to 170°C/325°F.

6 Whisk rind, juice, eggs, caster sugar and cream in a large bowl until combined. Strain mixture into pastry case.

7 Bake tart 35 minutes or until just set. Cool. Cover; refrigerate 3 hours or overnight.

8 Make candied blood oranges.

9 Stand tart at room temperature for 30 minutes before serving; top with half the candied oranges and a little syrup. Serve tart cut into slices with remaining candied oranges and syrup.

candied blood oranges Stir sugar, water and juice in a large frying pan over medium heat until sugar dissolves. Add orange slices; simmer, 20 minutes or until rind is soft. Add honey to pan; simmer a further 15 minutes or until oranges are candied and syrup is thickened.

prep + cook time 1 hours 50 minutes (+ refrigeration & cooling) **serves** 8

nutritional count per serving 31g total fat (15.8g saturated fat); 2740kJ (655 cal); 85.6g carbohydrate; 9.5g protein; 3.9g fibre

tips The tart can be made a day ahead. The candied blood oranges are best made close to serving.

IT'S NOT NECESSARY TO STIR MARMALADE DURING THE EARLY TO MIDDLE STAGES OF COOKING, HOWEVER TOWARDS THE END, AS IT NEARS JELLING POINT, A QUICK STIR WON'T HURT AND WILL LOOSEN ANY RIND THAT'S BEGINNING TO CATCH. PITH AND SEEDS CONTAIN PECTIN, WHICH IS WHY THEY ARE INCLUDED IN THE FRUIT MIXTURE.

MASTER FINE-CUT ORANGE MARMALADE

This basic method of making marmalade will work with most citrus fruits including grapefruit, lemons, tangerines and limes or various combinations of these fruits. However, for tangelo marmalade use 3 tangelos (630g) and 2 lemons (280g) as the fruit contains less pectin.

1kg (2 pounds) oranges

1.5 litres (6 cups) water

4½ cups (1kg) white (granulated) sugar, approximately

1 Using a wide-style vegetable peeler, peel rind without pith from oranges. Using a small knife, cut white pith from fruit following the curve of the fruit; reserve pith. Slice rind into thin strips. Quarter oranges; slice flesh thinly, reserve any seeds. Finely chop enough pith to tightly pack a ½ cup measuring cup. Place chopped pith and reserved seeds on a small square of muslin; tie into a bag.

2 Place rind, chopped flesh, muslin bag and the water in a large saucepan; bring to the boil. Reduce heat; simmer, covered, 1 hour or until rind is soft. Discard muslin bag.

3 Measure orange mixture; allow 1 cup (220g) sugar for each cup of orange mixture. Return orange mixture to pan with sugar; stir over high heat, without boiling, until sugar dissolves. Bring to the boil; boil, without stirring, for 30 minutes or until marmalade jells when tested on a chilled saucer (see tips).

4 Pour hot marmalade into hot sterilised jars (see tips); seal immediately. Label and date jars when cold.

prep + cook time 1 hour 45 minutes **makes** 4 cups

nutritional count per tablespoon 0g total fat (0g saturated fat); 368kJ (88 cal); 22.5g carbohydrate; 0.2g protein; 0.4g fibre

tips To test if marmalade has reached jelling point, place two small saucers in the freezer. Drop a spoonful of mixture on a chilled saucer; wait 30 second for the marmalade to cool and develop a skin. Push the marmalade with your finger, the skin will wrinkle if the marmalade is ready. If the marmalade is not jelling, return to the heat and boil it again for a few minutes, then repeat the test. If the marmalade refuses to set, try adding 2 tablespoons lemon juice. For information on sterilising jars, see page 236.

GARLIC

CHIVES
GREEN ONIONS
ASPARAGUS
BUK CHOY
BABY GREEN BEANS
BROAD BEANS
SPRING
CUCUMBERS
ARTICHOKES
SUGAR SNAP PEAS
MINT
LEEKS
PINEAPPLE

VEGETABLES

Spring beckons the plants to grow and they respond in kind. Young, tender shoots burst through the soil into a wondrous display. Make the most of all varieties of peas, asparagus and zucchini flowers.

FRUIT

The stepping stone to summer, spring sees fragrant fruits abound. Take pleasure in perfectly ripened pineapple and melons topped with fresh passionfruit – there's a burst of sunshine in every bite.

IT IS IMPORTANT TO USE THE FRESHEST FREE-RANGE EGGS YOU CAN FIND AS THEY WILL HOLD THEIR SHAPE WHILE POACHING.

LINGUINE PRIMAVERA & POACHED EGGS

180g (5½ ounces) shelled broad (fava) beans

100g (3 ounces) snow peas

2 teaspoons salt

500g (1 pound) linguine pasta

¼ cup (60ml) extra virgin olive oil

2 cloves garlic, sliced thinly

170g (5½ ounces) asparagus, cut into 5cm (2-inch) lengths

1 tablespoon white vinegar

4 eggs

¼ cup loosely packed fresh chervil leaves

1 cup (80g) finely grated parmesan

1 Place broad beans in a large saucepan of boiling water; boil 2 minutes or until just tender. Remove beans with a slotted spoon. Refresh under cold water; drain well. Add snow peas to same boiling water; boil 30 seconds or until bright green. Remove snow peas with a slotted spoon. Refresh under cold water; drain well. Remove grey skins from broad beans.

2 Return water to the boil; add salt. Cook pasta in boiling water for 8 minutes or until just tender; drain. Return to pan to keep warm.

3 Meanwhile, heat 1 tablespoon of the oil in a large frying pan over medium-high heat; cook garlic and asparagus, stirring, for 2 minutes or until softened. Stir in broad beans and snow peas. Remove from heat.

4 Bring water to the boil in a deep frying pan; add vinegar. Break 1 egg into a cup, then slide into pan. Repeat with remainin g eggs. When all eggs are in pan; return to the boil. Cover pan; remove from heat. Stand 3 minutes or until a light film of egg white sets over the eggs. Remove eggs with a slotted spoon; drain on paper towel.

5 Return vegetable mixture to heat, add remaining oil and pasta; toss until heated through. Season to taste.

6 Serve linguine topped with a poached egg, chervil, parmesan and freshly ground black pepper.

prep + cook time 30 minutes **serves** 4

nutritional count per serving 27.2g total fat (8.1g saturated fat); 3192kJ (763 cal); 91g carbohydrate; 33.3g protein; 8.7g fibre

tip You will need to buy about 750g (1½ pounds) broad beans in the pod for this recipe. Or, you can use 1½ cups (225g) frozen broad beans if you like.

ASPARAGUS, GRUYÈRE & PROSCIUTTO TART

20g (¾ ounce) butter

340g (11 ounces) asparagus, halved crossways

3 eggs

¾ cup (180ml) pouring cream

2 tablespoons coarsely chopped fresh chives

2 teaspoons fresh thyme leaves

¾ cup (90g) coarsely grated gruyère cheese

PARMESAN PASTRY

1¼ cups (185g) plain (all-purpose) flour

100g (3 ounces) cold butter, chopped

½ cup (40g) finely grated parmesan

1 egg yolk

1 tablespoon iced water, approximately

ASPARAGUS SALAD

480g (15½ ounces) green asparagus

440g (14 ounces) white asparagus

100g (3 ounces) thinly sliced prosciutto

2 tablespoons finely grated parmesan

50g (1½ ounces) drained marinated fetta, crumbled

1 Make parmesan pastry.

2 Oil a 12.5cm x 35cm (5-inch x 14-inch) rectangular loose-based tart tin. Roll pastry between sheets of baking paper until large enough to line tin. Ease pastry into tin, press into base and sides; trim edges. Place on an oven tray; refrigerate 30 minutes.

3 Preheat oven to 180°C/375°F.

4 Line pastry case with baking paper, fill with dried beans or rice. Bake 15 minutes. Remove paper and beans; bake a further 15 minutes. Increase oven to 200°C/400°F.

5 Meanwhile, melt butter in a medium frying pan; cook asparagus over medium heat, stirring, 5 minutes or until tender. Remove from pan. Whisk eggs, cream and herbs together in a large jug. Arrange asparagus in rows in pastry case, allowing the ends to stick out over the rim. Pour egg mixture over asparagus; sprinkle with gruyère.

6 Bake tart 30 minutes or until filling is just set. Stand 10 minutes.

7 Meanwhile, make asparagus salad.

8 Serve tart topped with asparagus salad.

parmesan pastry Process flour, butter and parmesan until crumbly. Add egg yolk and enough of the water to make ingredients come together. Turn dough onto a floured surface; knead gently until smooth. Wrap pastry in plastic; refrigerate 30 minutes.

asparagus salad Using a wide vegetable peeler or mandoline, peel green and white asparagus into long thin ribbons. Tear prosciutto slices into thirds. Place asparagus and prosciutto in a bowl with parmesan and fetta; toss gently to combine.

prep + cook time 1 hour 20 minutes (+ refrigeration) **serves** 6

nutritional count per serving 43.1g total fat (25.7g saturated fat); 2469kJ (590 cal); 25.2g carbohydrate; 24.1g protein; 4g fibre

INDIAN-SPICED LAMB WITH BEAN & COCONUT SALAD

1 tablespoon finely grated fresh ginger

1 clove garlic, crushed

1 tablespoon cumin seeds

1 teaspoon garam masala

⅓ cup (80ml) lemon juice

⅓ cup (80ml) olive oil

1kg (2 pounds) lamb rump steak,
   cut into 2.5cm (1-inch) cubes

¼ cup (35g) sunflower seed kernels

1 tablespoon sesame seeds

2 teaspoons brown mustard seeds

300g (9½ ounces) green beans,
   trimmed

300g (9½ ounces) yellow beans,
   trimmed

2 shallots (50g), sliced thinly

200g (6½ ounces) baby heirloom
   tomatoes, halved

¾ cup loosely packed fresh baby
   coriander (cilantro) leaves

2 tablespoons flaked coconut

1 cup (280g) Greek-style yoghurt

1 Combine ginger, garlic, spices, juice and oil in a large bowl; season to taste. Reserve 2 tablespoons of the ginger mixture.

2 Add lamb to ginger mixture in bowl; toss to coat. Thread lamb onto skewers; place in a shallow dish. Cover; refrigerate 30 minutes.

3 Meanwhile, toast seeds in a small frying pan over medium-low heat, stirring continuously until browned lightly. Remove from pan.

4 Cook green and yellow beans in a large saucepan of boiling salted water for 3 minutes or until tender; drain. Place beans in a medium bowl with the reserved ginger mixture, toasted seeds, shallots, tomatoes, coriander and coconut; toss gently to combine.

5 Cook lamb on heated oiled barbecue, turning occasionally, for 8 minutes or until browned all over and cooked as desired.

6 Serve lamb with bean salad and yoghurt.

prep + cook time 50 minutes (+ refrigeration) **serves** 4

nutritional count per serving 63g total fat (19.8g saturated fat); 3790kJ (905 cal); 18.5g carbohydrate; 63.1g protein; 8.2g fibre

tip Soak bamboo skewers for 30 minutes before use to prevent them scorching during cooking.

BAHARAT IS A MIDDLE EASTERN SPICE AVAILABLE FROM SOME DELIS AND MIDDLE EASTERN GROCERS. IF IT'S HARD TO FIND, USE MOROCCAN SPICE MIX INSTEAD WHICH IS READILY AVAILABLE FROM SUPERMARKETS. FALAFEL MIXTURE CAN BE SHAPED INTO BALLS INSTEAD OF OVALS. USE ROUNDED TABLESPOONS OF MIXTURE, PRESSING FIRMLY BEFORE GENTLY ROLLING INTO BALLS.

FALAFEL WITH TAHINI SAUCE

2.5kg (4 pounds) fresh broad (fava) beans in the pod

400g (12½ ounces) canned chickpeas (garbanzo beans), drained, rinsed

1 medium brown onion (150g), chopped coarsely

3 cloves garlic

1 cup coarsely chopped fresh coriander (cilantro)

1½ cups coarsely chopped fresh flat-leaf parsley

1 teaspoon fine salt

1 teaspoon baharat

2 teaspoons ground cumin

⅓ cup (50g) plain (all-purpose) flour

vegetable oil, for deep-frying

¼ cup fresh mint leaves

¼ teaspoon baharat, extra

TAHINI SAUCE

⅔ cup (180g) tahini

½ cup (125ml) lemon juice

⅓ cup (80ml) water

1 clove garlic, crushed

1 Shell broad beans. Place broad beans in a large saucepan of boiling water; boil 2 minutes or until just tender. Drain. Refresh under cold running water; drain well. Remove grey skins. You need 2 cups peeled broad beans for falafel and ½ cup reserved for serving.

2 Process 2 cups broad beans, chickpeas, onion, garlic, herbs, salt and spices until finely chopped. Shape mixture firmly into oval shapes. Place falafel on a tray lined with plastic wrap. Refrigerate 1 hour.

3 Meanwhile, make tahini sauce.

4 Coat falafel in flour; shake off excess. Fill a large saucepan one-third full with oil; heat to 180°C/350°C (or until a cube of bread browns in 10 seconds). Using a spoon, lower falafel in batches into oil, deep-fry, turning occasionally, 2 minutes or until browned; drain on paper towel.

5 Serve falafel with tahini sauce, reserved beans and mint leaves; sprinkle with extra baharat.

tahini sauce Whisk ingredients in a small bowl until smooth. Season to taste.

prep + cook time 50 minutes (+ standing & refrigeration) **serves 4**

nutritional count per serving 59.1g total fat (7.3g saturated fat); 3745kJ (895 cal); 26g carbohydrate; 45.2g protein; 43.5g fibre

tip You can use 750g (1½ pounds) frozen broad beans. Boil, refresh and remove skins as for fresh broad beans in step 1.

serving suggestion Serve with grilled flatbread.

ROAST BEEF, TUNA AÏOLI
& ARTICHOKES
(RECIPE PAGE 194)

ROAST BEEF, TUNA AÏOLI & ARTICHOKES

⅓ cup (80ml) olive oil

800g (1½ pounds) piece centre-cut beef eye fillet

6 medium globe artichokes (1.2kg)

¼ cup (60ml) lemon juice

½ cup (150g) aïoli

95g (3 ounces) canned tuna in oil, drained

5 anchovy fillets

1 small french bread stick (150g), sliced thinly

2 cloves garlic, sliced thinly

2 teaspoons baby capers

¼ cup loosely packed baby fresh flat-leaf parsley leaves

1 Preheat oven to 180°C/350°F.

2 Heat 1 tablespoon of the oil in a medium flameproof roasting dish over high heat; cook beef, turning, until browned all over. Season. Roast beef 30 minutes for medium. Transfer beef to a plate; cool. Cover; refrigerate 3 hours or overnight.

3 Meanwhile, snap off tough outer leaves from artichokes until you reach the tender inner yellow leaves. Using kitchen scissors, cut off the thorny tips from remaining leaves; trim stems then brush with 2 tablespoons of the juice. Place artichokes in a medium saucepan of water; bring to the boil. Simmer over medium heat 20 minutes or until almost tender. Drain; cool.

4 Process aïoli, tuna, anchovies and remaining juice until smooth. Season to taste.

5 Place bread on a baking-paper-lined large oven tray; brush with 1 tablespoon of the oil. Bake 10 minutes or until golden.

6 Meanwhile, cut artichokes in half; scoop out the hairy choke. Brush with 1 tablespoon of oil. Cook in a preheat chargrill pan for 2 minutes each side or until lightly charred.

7 Heat remaining oil in a small frying pan; cook garlic until lightly golden. Drain on paper towel.

8 Thinly slice beef; arrange on a platter, topped with tuna aïoli, garlic, capers and parsley. Serve with artichoke and toasts.

prep + cook time 1 hour 15 minutes (+ refrigeration) **serves** 6
nutritional count per serving 31.5g total fat (6.5g saturated fat); 2310kJ (552 cal); 20.9g carbohydrate; 40.4g protein; 12.2g fibre

(photograph page 193)

LAMB & SPINACH SAMOSAS

2 medium potatoes (400g), chopped finely

200g (6½ ounces) baby spinach leaves

1 tablespoon vegetable oil

1 medium brown onion (150g), chopped finely

5 cloves garlic, crushed

2 teaspoons finely grated fresh ginger

500g (1 pound) minced (ground) lamb

½ cup (150g) madras curry simmer sauce

1 tablespoon lemon juice

6 sheets puff pastry

1 egg, beaten lightly

1 Boil, steam or microwave potato until tender. Drain; cool.

2 Place spinach in a large heatproof bowl, cover with boiling water; stand 1 minute. Drain, then refresh under cold running water. Drain; squeeze out excess moisture from spinach and chop coarsely.

3 Heat oil in large frying pan over medium heat; cook onion, garlic and ginger, stirring, until soft. Add lamb; cook, stirring, over high heat, until browned. Stir in sauce; simmer 5 minutes. Stir in potato, spinach and juice; season to taste. Cool.

4 Preheat oven to 220°C/425°F. Line three large oven trays with baking paper.

5 Cut each pastry sheet into four squares. Place 2 tablespoons lamb mixture in centre of each pastry square. Brush pastry edges with egg. Fold pastry over filling to make triangles; press edges with a fork to seal.

6 Place triangles on trays; brush with egg. Bake 30 minutes or until golden.

prep + cook time 1 hour 15 minutes (+ cooling) **makes** 24
nutritional count per samosa 12.9g total fat (6.4g saturated fat); 931kJ (222 cal); 18g carbohydrate; 7.8g protein; 1.5g fibre

tips For children, choose a mild curry simmer sauce. You can also freeze the uncooked samosas before brushing with egg. Uncooked samosas can be baked from frozen.

serving suggestion Serve with Greek-style yoghurt, chutney, lemon wedges and coriander.

LAMB & SPINACH SAMOSAS

BAKED RICOTTA & SALSA VERDE WITH CHARGRILLED VEGETABLES

cooking oil spray

750g (1½ pounds) firm ricotta

1 free-range egg

¼ cup (20g) finely grated parmesan

¼ cup chopped fresh chives

¼ teaspoon dried chilli flakes

1 medium eggplant (440g),
    sliced thinly lengthways

2 medium red capsicums (bell peppers)
    (400g), cut into eight thick slices

2 medium zucchini (240g),
    sliced thinly lengthways

4 large marinated artichoke hearts,
    quartered

12 slices wholegrain sourdough bread
    (135g)

1 medium lemon (140g), rind removed
    with a zester

12 fresh small bay leaves

SALSA VERDE

1¾ cups lightly packed fresh
    basil leaves

2 cups lightly packed fresh
    flat-leaf parsley leaves

2 cloves garlic, crushed

2 anchovy fillets, chopped

2 teaspoons baby capers

1 teaspoon finely grated lemon rind

⅓ cup (80ml) extra virgin olive oil

2 teaspoons lemon juice

1 Preheat oven to 180°C/350°F. Spray a 12-hole (⅓-cup/80ml) muffin pan with cooking oil spray; line base and side of holes with baking paper.

2 Combine ricotta, egg, parmesan and chives in a large bowl; season. Spoon mixture into pan holes, level surface; sprinkle with chilli flakes.

3 Bake ricotta 20 minutes or until puffed and centre is firm. Stand in pan 5 minutes.

4 Meanwhile, make salsa verde.

5 Spray vegetables and bread slices with cooking oil spray; season vegetables. Cook vegetables on a heated chargrill plate (or barbecue or grill) over medium-high heat for 2 minutes each side or until charred and tender. Place bread on chargrill plate for 1 minute each side or until lightly charred.

6 Place baked ricotta on a platter; top with salsa verde, lemon zest and bay leaves. Serve with vegetables and bread.

salsa verde Process herbs, garlic, anchovy, capers, rind and half the oil until mixture is coarsely chopped. With motor operating, add remaining oil in a thin stream until mixture is smooth. Transfer mixture to a small bowl, stir in juice; season to taste. Cover surface with plastic wrap.

prep + cook time 1 hour serves 6

nutritional count per serving 25.8g total fat (9.4g saturated fat); 1690kJ (404 cal); 18.7g carbohydrate; 19.5g protein; 10.7g fibre

tip You can also make a whole baked ricotta in an 18cm (7¼-inch) springform pan. Oil pan, then line base and side with baking paper. Bake ricotta for 35 minutes or until puffed and centre is firm.

THIS SOUP IS BEST MADE JUST BEFORE SERVING AS THE GREEN VEGETABLES WILL LOSE THEIR VIBRANCY ON STANDING. IF YOU CAN'T FIND ZUCCHINI FLOWERS, USE A MEDIUM-SIZED ZUCCHINI SLICED THINLY INSTEAD.

PRIMAVERA SOUP WITH PANGRATTATO

250g (8 ounces) zucchini flowers, with zucchini attached

30g (1 ounce) butter

4 shallots (100g), chopped

1 litre (4 cups) vegetable stock

2 cups (500ml) water

⅓ cup (75g) risoni pasta

150g (4½ ounces) asparagus, cut into 3cm (1¼-inch) lengths

2 cups (240g) frozen baby peas

1 teaspoon finely grated lemon rind

PANGRATTATO

200g (6½ ounces) crusty italian bread

2 tablespoons extra virgin olive oil

1 fresh long red chilli, chopped finely

2 cloves garlic, chopped

⅓ cup loosely packed small fresh flat-leaf parsley leaves

1 teaspoon finely grated lemon rind

1 Snap off flowers from zucchini; remove the yellow stamens from the centre of each flower. Cut zucchini in half lengthways.

2 Heat butter in a large saucepan over medium heat; cook shallots, stirring, for 3 minutes or until soft.

3 Add stock and the water to pan; bring to the boil. Add pasta and zucchini; simmer, 5 minutes, stirring occasionally.

4 Meanwhile, make pangrattato.

5 Add asparagus and peas to soup; simmer, 5 minutes or until just tender. Season to taste. Stir in zucchini flowers.

6 Ladle soup into bowls; top with pangrattato and rind.

pangrattato Remove crust from bread; tear bread into 1cm (½-inch) pieces. Heat oil in a large frying pan over medium-high heat; cook chilli and bread pieces, stirring, until browned lightly and crisp. Add garlic; cook until fragrant. Remove from heat; stir in parsley and rind. Season to taste.

prep + cook time 25 minutes **serves** 4

nutritional count per serving 17.7g total fat (5.9g saturated fat); 1760kJ (420 cal); 46.7g carbohydrate; 14.3g protein; 9.2g fibre

tip Pangrattato is the Italian name for breadcrumbs, which can be fine or coarse, these are best made with day-old bread.

PEA, FENNEL & SPINACH LASAGNE

1 medium bulb fennel (300g), trimmed, feathery fronds reserved

¼ cup (60ml) extra virgin olive oil

2 cloves garlic, crushed

2 shallots (50g), chopped finely

1 teaspoon ground fennel

2 teaspoons finely grated lemon rind

500g (1 pound) english spinach, trimmed

1½ cups (240g) fresh peas

1.2kg (2½ pounds) canned chopped tomatoes

1 cup roughly torn fresh basil leaves

250g (8 ounces) wholemeal lasagne sheets

¼ cup (60g) soft ricotta

2 tablespoons extra virgin olive oil, extra

¼ cup small basil leaves, extra

RICOTTA BÉCHAMEL

1¾ cups (420g) soft ricotta

3 free-range eggs

½ cup (140g) Greek-style yoghurt

¼ cup (60ml) lemon juice

1 cup (200g) crumbled fetta

½ cup (125ml) sparkling mineral water

1 Finely chop the fennel. Reserve 2 tablespoons of the feathery fronds to serve.

2 Heat 1½ tablespoons of the oil in a large frying pan over medium heat; cook fennel, garlic, shallots and ground fennel, stirring, for 8 minutes or until lightly golden. Transfer mixture to a large bowl; stir in rind. Season to taste.

3 Wash spinach leaves but don't dry. Cook spinach in same pan over high heat, in two batches, until wilted; drain. When cool enough to handle, squeeze out excess liquid. Coarsely chop spinach; stir into fennel mixture. Season to taste. Refrigerate until cooled. Stir in peas.

4 Preheat oven to 200°C/400°F.

5 Combine tomatoes, basil and remaining oil in a bowl; season.

6 Make ricotta béchamel.

7 Spread one-third of the tomato mixture over the base of a 3-litre (12-cup) baking dish. Cover with one-third of the pasta sheets. Top with half the spinach mixture and half the béchamel. Continue layering with remaining pasta sheets, tomato mixture, spinach mixture and béchamel, finishing with pasta sheets and tomato mixture. Top with spoonfuls of ricotta.

8 Bake lasagne for 45 minutes or until top is golden and pasta is cooked (cover with greased foil if necessary to prevent overbrowning). Stand for 10 minutes before serving. Serve lasagne drizzled with extra oil and topped with extra basil and reserved fennel fronds.

ricotta béchamel Whisk ricotta, eggs, yoghurt, juice and fetta in a large bowl until combined. Whisk mineral water into mixture until combined.

prep + cook time 1 hour 10 minutes (+ cooling) **serves** 6

nutritional count per serving 35g total fat (13.5g saturated fat); 2637kJ (630 cal); 43.6g carbohydrate; 29.3g protein; 11.8g fibre

tip You can also layer the lasagne in a large deep 3-litre (12-cup) ovenproof frying pan.

GREEN BARLEY SALAD
(RECIPE PAGE 204)

FROZEN EDAMAME, SOY BEANS IN THE POD, ARE AVAILABLE FROM ASIAN SUPERMARKETS. YOU WILL NEED ABOUT 300G (9½ OUNCES) IN THE POD IF YOU CAN'T FIND SHELLED EDAMAME. YOU CAN ALSO USE FROZEN BROAD (FAVA) BEANS; YOU'LL NEED TO DISCARD THE OUTER SKINS AFTER THE PODDED BEANS HAVE BEEN BROUGHT TO THE BOIL.

GREEN BARLEY SALAD

1 cup (200g) pearl barley

1 cup (120g) frozen peas

1 cup (150g) shelled edamame

150g (4½ ounces) snow peas, sliced thinly

2 green onions (scallions), sliced thinly

½ cup loosely packed fresh mint leaves

2 tablespoons extra virgin olive oil

1 tablespoon lemon juice

335g (10½ ounces) labne in olive oil, drained

1 Cook barley in a medium saucepan of salted water over medium heat for 25 minutes or until tender. Drain; rinse under cold water until cold. Drain well.

2 Meanwhile, bring a medium saucepan of salted water to the boil. Add peas, edamame and snow peas; boil for 1 minute. Drain; place in a bowl of iced water until cold. Drain well.

3 Place barley and pea mixture in a shallow serving dish with green onion and mint; drizzle with combined oil and juice. Toss gently to combine. Season to taste.

4 Serve salad topped with labne.

prep + cook time 30 minutes serves 6

nutritional count per serving 20.9g total fat (2.9g saturated fat); 1448kJ (346 cal); 28.6g carbohydrate; 9.3g protein; 6.4g fibre

(photograph page 202)

QUINOA, CHICKEN & PARSLEY SALAD

½ cup (100g) red or white quinoa

1 cup (250ml) water

⅓ cup (80ml) lemon juice

¼ cup (60ml) extra virgin olive oil

250g (8 ounces) cherry tomatoes, halved

1½ cups loosely packed fresh flat-leaf parsley leaves

1 cup loosely packed fresh mint leaves

3 green onions (scallions), sliced thinly lengthways

1½ cups (250g) shredded barbecued chicken

1 Place quinoa and the water in a small saucepan; bring to the boil. Reduce heat; simmer, covered, 10 minutes or until water is absorbed and quinoa is tender. Remove from heat.

2 Combine juice and oil in a large bowl; season. Add quinoa, tomato, herbs, onion and chicken; toss gently to combine.

prep + cook time 20 minutes serves 4 (as a light lunch)

nutritional count per serving 19.2g total fat (3.4g saturated fat); 1188kJ (284 cal); 7.4g carbohydrate; 19.2g protein; 1.8g fibre

tip You need about half a barbecued chicken for this recipe.

ONLY 'TRUE' TARRAGON, THE FRENCH VARIETY; HAS A LOVELY ANISE-LIKE FLAVOUR THAT PAIRS WELL WITH SEAFOOD. ALTHOUGH RARELY LABELLED, FRENCH TARRAGON HAS DISTINGUISHING NARROW LEAVES, WHILE RUSSIAN TARRAGON HAS SERRATED LEAVES AND YELLOW FLOWERS.

PRAWN, PEA & BROAD BEAN FRITTATA

½ cup fresh flat-leaf parsley leaves

⅓ cup fresh dill sprigs

¼ cup fresh tarragon leaves

6 free-range eggs

½ cup (125ml) buttermilk

2 tablespoons dried breadcrumbs

500g (1 pound) cooked medium
prawns (shrimp)

2 tablespoons olive oil

2 medium zucchini (240g), halved
lengthways, sliced thinly

3 green onions (scallions), sliced thinly

2 cloves garlic, crushed

2 cups (240g) frozen peas, thawed

2¼ cups (370g) frozen broad (fava)
beans, thawed, peeled

1 medium lemon (140g), segmented
(see tips)

1 tablespoon baby salted capers, rinsed

⅓ cup (80g) ricotta, crumbled

1 Coarsely chop half the parsley, dill and tarragon. Reserve remaining herbs.

2 Whisk chopped herbs with eggs, buttermilk and breadcrumbs in a large bowl; season.

3 Shell and devein prawns, leaving 6 prawns with tails intact.

4 Preheat oven to 180°C/350°F.

5 Heat oil in a 21cm (8½-inch) ovenproof frying pan over medium heat; cook zucchini and green onion, stirring, for 5 minutes or until soft. Add garlic, peas and beans; cook, stirring, 1 minute or until fragrant. Add egg mixture; gently shake pan to distribute mixture. Cook over low-medium heat, without stirring, 5 minutes or until edge is set. Add prawns, placing prawns with tails upright in pan. Bake frittata 20 minutes or until the centre is just firm.

6 Meanwhile, combine reserved herbs, lemon segments and capers in a small bowl.

7 Serve frittata topped with lemon herb mixture and ricotta.

prep + cook time 1 hour **serves** 4

nutritional count per serving 20.6g total fat (5.6g saturated fat); 1733kJ (414 cal); 15.8g carbohydrate; 35.8g protein; 10.4g fibre

tips To segment the lemon, use a small sharp knife to cut the top and bottom from lemon. Cut off the rind with the white pith, following the curve of the fruit. Holding the lemon over a bowl, cut down both sides of the white membrane to release each segment. If you don't have an ovenproof frying pan, wrap the handle of your pan in several layers of foil to protect it. You can also cook the frittata in an oiled 21cm (8½-inch) round ovenproof dish. Cook the vegetables in step 5 in a frying pan, then transfer to the dish; add egg mixture, prawns and ricotta. Cook in the oven for 25 minutes or until set.

SKORDALIA IS A CLASSIC GREEK ACCOMPANIMENT TO MEAT, MADE FROM EITHER POTATO OR BREAD PUREED WITH A LARGE AMOUNT OF GARLIC PLUS OLIVE OIL, LEMON JUICE OR VINEGAR, HERBS AND, OCCASIONALLY, GROUND NUTS.

GREEK ROAST LAMB WITH SKORDALIA & LEMON POTATOES

2 cloves garlic, crushed

½ cup (125ml) lemon juice

2 tablespoons olive oil

1 tablespoon fresh oregano leaves

1 teaspoon fresh lemon thyme leaves

2kg (4-pound) lamb leg

5 large potatoes (1.5kg), quartered

1 medium lemon (140g), rind peeled into strips

2 tablespoons lemon juice

2 tablespoons olive oil, extra

8 sprigs fresh lemon thyme, extra

SKORDALIA

1 medium potato (200g), quartered

3 cloves garlic, quartered

1 tablespoon lemon juice

1 tablespoon white wine vinegar

2 tablespoons water

⅓ cup (80ml) olive oil

1 tablespoon warm water

1 Combine garlic, juice, oil, oregano and thyme leaves in a large bowl; add lamb, turn to coat well. Cover; refrigerate 3 hours or overnight.

2 Preheat oven to 160°C/325°F

3 Place lamb in a large roasting pan; roast, uncovered, 4 hours.

4 Meanwhile, make skordalia.

5 Combine potatoes, rind, juice and extra oil in a large bowl; place, in a single layer, on an oven tray. Roast potato, for the last 30 minutes of lamb cooking time.

6 Remove lamb from oven; cover to keep warm.

7 Increase oven to 220°C/425°F; roast potatoes a further 20 minutes or until golden. Serve lamb and potatoes with skordalia; top with extra thyme.

skordalia Boil, steam or microwave potato until tender; drain. Push potato through a ricer or fine sieve into a large bowl; cool 10 minutes. Add garlic, juice, vinegar and the water to potato; stir until well combined. Place potato mixture in blender; with motor operating, gradually add oil in a thin, steady stream, blending only until skordalia thickens (do not overmix or the sauce will become gluey). Stir in the water.

prep + cook time 5 hours (+ refrigeration) serves 4

nutritional count per serving 57g total fat (14g saturated fat); 4556kJ (1090 cal); 51.5g carbohydrate; 91.2g protein; 6.7g fibre

STEAK WITH CASHEW NAM JIM & ASIAN GREENS

800g (1½ pounds) thick-cut
   rump steak

1 tablespoon peanut oil

350g (11 ounces) gai lan

270g (8½ ounces) baby pak choy or
   buk choy, trimmed, quartered

100g (3 ounces) snow peas

4 green onions (scallions),
   sliced thinly

¼ cup (40g) unsalted roasted cashews,
   chopped coarsely

¼ cup loosely packed fresh coriander
   (cilantro) sprigs

CASHEW NAM JIM

2 shallots (50g), chopped

2 cloves garlic

3 fresh long green chillies,
   seeded, chopped

2 fresh coriander (cilantro) roots,
   chopped

1 teaspoon finely grated fresh ginger

2 tablespoons grated dark palm sugar

⅓ cup (50g) unsalted roasted cashews

⅓ cup (80ml) lime juice,
   approximately

1 tablespoon fish sauce, approximately

1 Make cashew nam jim.

2 Trim fat from steak; rub steak with oil, season. Cook steak on a heated chargrill plate (or barbecue or grill) on medium-high heat for 4 minutes each side for medium or until done as desired. Remove steak from heat; cover with foil, rest 5 minutes.

3 Meanwhile, trim gai lan stalks; cut stalks from leaves. Steam stalks, in a single layer, in a large steamer over a wok or large saucepan of boiling water for 1 minute. Place separated pak choy on top; steam a further 2 minutes. Add snow peas and gai lan leaves; steam a further 2 minutes or until vegetables are just tender.

4 Place vegetables on a platter in layers, top with thickly sliced steak; drizzle with steak resting juices. Spoon nam jim on steak; top with green onion, nuts and coriander.

cashew nam jim Blend shallots, garlic, chilli, coriander root, ginger, sugar and cashews (or pound with a mortar and pestle) until mixture forms a paste. Transfer to a small bowl; stir in juice and fish sauce to taste.

prep + cook time 40 minutes **serves** 4

nutritional count per serving 35g total fat (9.7g saturated fat); 2888kJ (670 cal); 14g carbohydrate; 76.4g protein; 7.4g fibre

tips You will need about 3 limes for this recipe. Nam jim can be made a day ahead; keep tightly covered in the fridge until ready to use.

serving suggestion Serve with steamed jasmine or brown rice.

The welcoming warmth of spring makes us venture outside amid the new growth and cheerful blossoms. It's the perfect time to grab a picnic blanket for a relaxing afternoon on the lawn with friends.

BAKED SALMON WITH TAHINI SAUCE & TABBOULEH

700g (1½ pound) piece salmon fillet, skin-on, pin-boned

1½ teaspoons sumac

2 tablespoons extra virgin olive oil

TABBOULEH

1 cup firmly packed small fresh flat-leaf parsley leaves

¼ cup firmly packed small fresh mint leaves

2 green onions (scallions), sliced thinly

½ cup (80g) coarse cracked wheat

1½ cups (375ml) water

200g (6½ ounces) heirloom tomatoes, quartered

1 tablespoon lemon juice

TAHINI SAUCE

½ cup (140g) Greek-style yoghurt

1½ tablespoons tahini

1 clove garlic, crushed

2 teaspoons lemon juice

1 Make tabbouleh, then tahini sauce.

2 Preheat oven to 200°C/400°F.

3 Line an oven tray with baking paper. Place salmon on tray; sprinkle with 1 teaspoon of the sumac, then drizzle with oil. Season. Bake for 20 minutes or until salmon is almost cooked through.

4 Top salmon with reserved herb mixture and remaining sumac; serve with tahini sauce and tabbouleh.

tabbouleh Combine herbs and green onion in a large bowl; reserve half the mixture for serving. Bring cracked wheat and the water to the boil in a small saucepan. Reduce heat to low; cook 20 minutes or until tender. Drain. Add cracked wheat to large bowl with tomatoes and juice; toss gently to combine. Season.

tahini sauce Whisk ingredients in a small bowl until combined; season to taste.

prep + cook time 50 minutes **serves** 4

nutritional count per serving 39.6g total fat (9.4g saturated fat); 2773kJ (663 cal); 14g carbohydrate; 59.4g protein; 7.4g fibre

tip You can make the tabbouleh and tahini sauce several hours ahead; refrigerate, covered, until ready to use.

PASSIONFRUIT CAKE
WITH ORANGE BLOSSOM SYRUP
(RECIPE PAGE 218)

PASSIONFRUIT CAKE WITH ORANGE BLOSSOM SYRUP

220g (7 ounces) unsalted butter, softened

1 cup (220g) caster (superfine) sugar

3 eggs

2 cups (300g) self-raising flour

⅔ cup (160ml) buttermilk

⅓ cup (80ml) passionfruit pulp

ORANGE BLOSSOM SYRUP

1 peppermint tea bag

1 cup (250ml) boiling water

1 cup (220g) caster (superfine) sugar

½ cup (125ml) passionfruit pulp

1 teaspoon orange blossom water

1 Make orange blossom syrup.

2 Preheat oven to 180°C/350°F. Grease a 12cm x 23cm (4¾-inch x 9¼-inch) loaf pan; line base with baking paper.

3 Beat butter and sugar in a medium bowl with an electric mixer 6 minutes or until pale and fluffy. Beat in eggs, one at a time. Fold in flour, then buttermilk in alternate batches; fold in passionfruit until just combined. Spoon mixture into pan; level surface.

4 Bake cake 50 minutes or until a skewer inserted into the centre comes out clean. Stand cake in pan 10 minutes before turning, top-side up, onto a wire rack to cool.

5 Place cake on a platter. Serve cake cut into slices drizzled with syrup and cream, if you like.

orange blossom syrup Place tea bag in a small saucepan, pour over boiling water; steep 5 minutes. Squeeze liquid from tea bag; discard bag. Add sugar and passionfruit pulp to tea; stir over low heat until sugar dissolves. Increase heat to high; bring to the boil, boil 15 minutes or until thick and syrupy. Remove from heat; stir in orange blossom water. Cool.

prep + cook time 1 hour 45 minutes (+ standing & cooling)
serves 8

nutritional count per serving 25.3g total fat (10.7g saturated fat); 2469kJ (590 cal); 84g carbohydrate; 7.8g protein; 2.8g fibre

tip You will need about 12 passionfruit for this recipe.

(photograph page 217)

BANANA & WALNUT CAKE WITH SALTED CARAMEL CREAM

125g (4 ounces) butter, softened, chopped

¾ cup (165g) firmly packed brown sugar

2 eggs

1½ cups (225g) self-raising flour

½ teaspoon bicarbonate of soda (baking soda)

1 teaspoon ground cinnamon

1½ cups (360g) mashed ripe banana

½ cup (120g) sour cream

1¼ cups (125g) walnut halves, roasted, chopped

3 teaspoons espresso coffee granules

¼ cup (60ml) boiling water

1 teaspoon sea salt flakes

CARAMEL CREAM

250g (8 ounces) mascarpone

250g (8 ounces) bottled dulce de leche

1 Preheat oven to 180°C/350°F. Grease a deep 20cm (8-inch) round cake pan; line base with baking paper.

2 Beat butter and sugar in a small bowl with an electric mixer until pale and fluffy. Beat in eggs, one at a time, until just combined. Transfer mixture to a large bowl. Stir in sifted dry ingredients with mashed banana, sour cream, 1 cup (100g) nuts and combined coffee and water. Spoon mixture into pan.

3 Bake cake for 1 hour or until a skewer inserted into the centre comes out clean. Stand cake in pan for 5 minutes before turning, top-side up, onto a wire rack to cool.

4 Meanwhile, make caramel cream.

5 Just before serving, spread caramel cream on top of cooled cake. Decorate with remaining nuts and the salt flakes.

caramel cream Stir mascarpone and dulce de leche in a small bowl with a wooden spoon until combined and spreadable.

prep + cook time 1 hour 30 minutes (+ cooling) **serves** 12

nutritional count per serving 30.3g total fat (13.7g saturated fat); 2036kJ (486 cal); 42.9g carbohydrate; 7.7g protein; 2.2g fibre

tip Dulce de leche is a rich milk-based caramel sauce/spread available from some supermarkets and delis.

BANANA & WALNUT CAKE WITH
SALTED CARAMEL CREAM

PASSIONFRUIT TART WITH ORANGE MASCARPONE CREAM

1 cup (150g) plain (all-purpose) flour

½ cup (80g) pure icing (confectioners') sugar

75g (2½ ounces) cold unsalted butter, chopped coarsely

1 egg yolk

1 teaspoon vanilla extract

1 tablespoon iced water

⅔ cup (160ml) passionfruit pulp

300ml pouring cream

½ cup (110g) caster (superfine) sugar

4 eggs

ORANGE MASCARPONE CREAM

250g (8 ounces) mascarpone

¼ cup (60ml) thick (double) cream

2 tablespoons icing (confectioners') sugar

2 tablespoons finely grated orange rind

1 Process flour, pure icing sugar and butter until crumbly. Add egg yolk, extract and the water; process until ingredients just come together. Wrap pastry in plastic wrap; refrigerate 30 minutes.

2 Grease a 26cm (10½-inch) round loose-based fluted tart tin. Roll pastry between sheets of baking paper until large enough to line tin. Lift pastry into tin, ease into base and side; trim edge. Prick base all over with a fork. Cover; refrigerate 20 minutes.

3 Preheat oven to 200°C/400°F.

4 Place pan on an oven tray. Line pastry with baking paper; fill with dried beans or rice. Bake 10 minutes; remove paper and beans. Bake a further 10 minutes or until pastry is golden. Cool.

5 Meanwhile, reserve ¼ cup of the passionfruit pulp. Strain remaining pulp; reserve 2 tablespoons of the seeds. Whisk cream, sugar and eggs together in a medium bowl; stir in strained passionfruit juice and reserved seeds.

6 Reduce oven to 170°C/340°F. Pour cream mixture into pastry case. Bake 35 minutes or until just set. Cool; refrigerate 3 hours or overnight.

7 Make orange mascarpone cream.

8 Serve tart topped with mascarpone cream; drizzled with reserved passionfruit pulp.

orange mascarpone cream Combine ingredients in a small bowl.

prep + cook time 1 hour 30 minutes (+ refrigeration & cooling) **serves** 8

nutritional count per serving 39.4g total fat (23.6g saturated fat); 2353kJ (562 cal); 43.4g carbohydrate; 8.8g protein; 3.7g fibre

tip You need about 10 passionfruit for this recipe.

PINEAPPLE & CARDAMOM TARTE TARTIN

1 medium ripe pineapple (1.25kg)

90g (3 ounces) butter, chopped

¾ cup (165g) firmly packed brown sugar

½ teaspoon ground cinnamon

½ teaspoon ground ginger

¼ teaspoon ground cardamom

pinch of ground cloves

1 sheet butter puff pastry

2 tablespoons fresh mint leaves

1 Preheat oven to 200°C/400°F. Line a 26cm (10½-inch) heavy-based ovenproof frying pan (23cm/9¼-inch base measure) with baking paper.

2 Trim top and bottom from pineapple; remove the skin. Cut pineapple into 5mm (¼-inch) thick slices. Using a small pastry cutter, cut the core from each slice.

3 Stir butter, sugar and spices in a large frying pan over medium heat until sugar dissolves. Add half the pineapple slices, bring to a simmer; cook, turning pineapple, for 3 minutes or until just tender. Using a slotted spoon, transfer pineapple to a tray; cool. Repeat with remaining pineapple. Reserve syrup in pan.

4 Arrange pineapple slices slightly overlapping in lined frying pan. Combine any standing juices on the tray from the pineapple with reserved syrup. Cut a 26cm (10½-inch) round from pastry sheet; place on pineapple, tucking the edge in around the pineapple.

5 Bake tart for 25 minutes or until pastry is puffed, cooked through and golden. Stand in pan 10 minutes. Carefully invert tart onto a rimmed platter; lift away the lining paper.

6 Reheat reserved syrup over medium heat for 2 minutes or until thickened slightly. Drizzle or brush syrup over pineapple. Serve immediately topped with mint leaves.

prep + cook time 1 hour **serves** 6

nutritional count per serving 18.4g total fat (9.4g saturated fat); 1509kJ (361 cal); 46.2g carbohydrate; 2.2g protein; 2.2g fibre

serving suggestion Serve with vanilla ice-cream.

PINEAPPLE SALAD WITH MACADAMIA & COCONUT PRALINE

4 kaffir lime leaves, shredded finely

⅓ cup (80ml) lime juice

¼ cup (60ml) white rum

2 medium red papaya (1.5kg), halved, seeded, sliced thinly

3 medium oranges (720g), segmented (see tips)

1 medium pineapple (1.25kg), cored, sliced thinly

30g (1 ounce) flaked coconut, toasted lightly

MACADAMIA & COCONUT PRALINE

50g (1½ ounces) macadamia halves, roasted lightly

30g (1 ounce) flaked coconut, toasted lightly

1 cup (220g) caster (superfine) sugar

½ cup (125ml) water

3 star anise

1 Make macadamia and coconut praline.

2 Combine lime leaves, juice and rum in a small jug.

3 Layer fruit and half the praline in a large bowl, drizzling with rum mixture as you layer. Cover; refrigerate 30 minutes.

4 Serve pineapple salad topped with remaining praline and flaked coconut.

macadamia & coconut praline Spread macadamia and coconut, in a single layer, on a greased oven tray. Combine sugar, the water and star anise in a small, heavy-based saucepan; stir over low heat, without boiling, until sugar dissolves. Increase heat; boil, without stirring until mixture is just beginning to turn golden. Remove star anise; cook a few more seconds until syrup turns a caramel colour. Remove from heat; pour over nuts and coconut. Cool until hard. Break into 4cm (1½-inch) shards.

prep + cook time 40 minutes (+ standing) **serves** 10

nutritional count per serving 9.1g total fat (4.4g saturated fat); 1123kJ (268 cal); 40.6g carbohydrate; 2.4g protein; 5.9g fibre

tip To segment the oranges, use a small sharp knife to cut the top and bottom from each orange. Cut off the rind with the white pith, following the curve of the fruit. Holding each orange over a bowl, cut down both sides of the white membrane to release each segment.

TO MAKE THIS A HEALTHY DESSERT, WE USED LOGICANE A LOW GI FORM OF CASTER SUGAR. IT IS AVAILABLE FROM MOST MAJOR SUPERMARKETS. FOR LEMON STRIPS, USE A VEGETABLE PEELER TO PEEL WIDE STRIPS AND AVOID TAKING OFF TOO MUCH OF THE WHITE PITH WITH THE RIND AS IT IS BITTER. THE SYRUP CAN BE MADE 4 HOURS AHEAD AND COMBINED WITH THE ORANGES; REFRIGERATE, COVERED UNTIL NEEDED.

BLOOD ORANGE & LEMON YOGHURT CUPS

1 vanilla bean

⅓ cup (75g) low GI caster (superfine) sugar (see note above)

½ cup (125ml) water

4 wide strips lemon rind

1 tablespoon lemon juice

2 blood oranges (360g), peeled, sliced

2 medium oranges (480g), peeled, sliced

3 cups (840g) Greek-style yoghurt

¼ cup loosely packed fresh mint leaves

1 Split vanilla bean in half lengthways; scrape seeds into a small saucepan. Add vanilla bean to pan with sugar, the water and rind; bring to the boil. Reduce heat; simmer 6 minutes or until syrup has thickened slightly. Cool. Discard vanilla bean; stir in juice.

2 Combine orange slices and sugar syrup in a medium bowl.

3 Spoon yoghurt into four 1¼ cup (310ml) serving glasses; top with oranges, syrup and rind. Serve topped with mint.

prep + cook time 45 minutes serves 4

nutritional count per serving 12.7g total fat (8g saturated fat); 1756kJ (419 cal); 59.7g carbohydrate; 12.4g protein; 4.5g fibre

LIME, PASSIONFRUIT & LEMON GRASS FROZEN YOGHURT CAKE

You will need to make this recipe the day before.

¾ cup (110g) plain (all-purpose) flour

¼ cup (35g) self-raising flour

½ teaspoon bicarbonate of soda (baking soda)

2 teaspoons finely grated lime rind

⅓ cup (90g) firmly packed grated palm sugar

60g (2 ounces) butter

⅓ cup (115g) golden syrup or treacle

1 egg

½ cup (125ml) buttermilk

1½ cups (420g) Greek-style yoghurt

300ml thickened (heavy) cream

⅔ cup (160ml) passionfruit pulp

CANDIED LIME

1½ cups (305g) firmly packed grated palm sugar

½ cup (125ml) water

2 tablespoons lime juice

1 stalk fresh lemon grass, quartered, bruised

4 limes, sliced thinly

1 Make candied lime.

2 Preheat oven to 170°C/340°F. Grease a 26cm x 32cm (10½-inch x 12¾-inch) swiss roll pan; line base and long sides with baking paper, extending the paper 5cm (2 inches) over the sides.

3 Sift flours and soda into a medium bowl; stir in rind. Place sugar, butter and golden syrup in a small saucepan; stir over low heat until sugar dissolves. Stir warm butter mixture, egg and buttermilk into flour mixture. Pour mixture into pan.

4 Bake cake 12 minutes or until cake springs back when pressed lightly with a finger and shrinks away from side of pan slightly. Brush warm cake with 2 tablespoons of the reserved candied lime syrup. Cool in pan.

5 Line the base and sides of a deep 14cm x 23cm (5½-inch x 9¼-inch) loaf pan with baking paper.

6 Beat yoghurt and cream in a small bowl with an electric mixer until soft peaks form; fold in all but 1 tablespoon of the remaining reserved candied lime syrup and half the passionfruit pulp. Pour a little more than one-third of yoghurt mixture into loaf pan (this will be about 1½ cups of mixture). Trim a 12cm x 22cm (4¾-inch x 9-inch) piece from half the cake; carefully place in pan over yoghurt. Cover; freeze 1 hour or until firm. Refrigerate remaining yoghurt mixture. Cover remaining cake.

7 Pour remaining yoghurt mixture into pan. Trim a 14cm x 23cm (5½-inch x 9¼-inch) piece from remaining cake; carefully place on yoghurt layer. Cover pan; freeze 3 hours or overnight.

8 Turn cake onto a platter; stand 10 minutes before serving. Just before serving, top with lime slices. Combine remaining tablespoon of reserved candied lime syrup with remaining passionfruit pulp; drizzle over cake.

candied lime Stir palm sugar, the water, juice and lemon grass in a medium heavy-based saucepan over low heat, without boiling, until sugar dissolves. Bring to the boil. Reduce heat; simmer, for 3 minutes or until syrup is reduced. Remove from heat; add lime slices, leave to cool in syrup. Drain lime slices; reserve slices and syrup separately. Discard lemon grass.

prep + cook time 1 hour 15 minutes (+ cooling & freezing) **serves** 12

nutritional count per serving 16.3g total fat (9.4g saturated fat); 1613kJ (385 cal); 55.1g carbohydrate; 5.2g protein; 2.4g fibre

tips You will need about 8 passionfruit for this recipe. You can substitute canned passionfruit pulp, if you like, however to compensate for the sugar added during canning add a teaspoon or two of lime juice. This recipe can be made up to 1 week ahead; cover tightly with foil, then freeze.

BANOFFEE MERINGUE WITH HONEYCOMB

4 egg whites

¼ teaspoon cream of tartar

¼ cup (55g) caster (superfine) sugar

¾ cup (165g) firmly packed
  brown sugar

2 teaspoons cornflour (cornstarch)

1 teaspoon white vinegar

¼ teaspoon vanilla extract

2 medium bananas (400g), sliced

1 tablespoon caster (superfine) sugar,
  extra

300ml thick (double) cream (56% fat)

100g (3 ounces) honeycomb,
  chopped coarsely

DULCE DE LECHE

395g (12½ ounces) canned sweetened
  condensed milk

1 Make dulce de leche.

2 Preheat oven to 120°C/250°F. Line two large oven trays with baking paper. Mark a 24cm (9½-inch) round on each piece of paper; turn, marked-side down, on trays.

3 Beat egg whites, cream of tartar and sugars in a medium bowl with an electric mixer on high speed for 8 minutes or until thick and glossy and sugar is dissolved. Beat in cornflour, vinegar and extract on low speed. Divide mixture evenly between trays, spreading to cover just inside marked rounds and swirling meringue.

4 Bake meringues for 1 hour or until dry to touch. Cool in oven with door ajar.

5 Place banana slices, in a single layer, on an oven tray; sprinkle with extra caster sugar. Using a blowtorch, caramelise sugar.

6 Whisk dulce de leche in a medium bowl until smooth. Whisk cream in a small bowl until soft peaks form.

7 Place one meringue on a platter. Spread one-third of the cream on meringue. Drop spoonfuls of half the dulce de leche on cream. Repeat layering with remaining meringue, another one-third cream and remaining dulce de leche. Top dulce de leche with remaining cream, banana slices and honeycomb.

dulce de leche Preheat oven to 220°C/425°F. Pour condensed milk into a 1.5-litre (6-cup) ceramic ovenproof dish. Cover dish tightly with foil; crush excess foil upwards. Place ceramic dish in a medium baking dish; add enough boiling water to come halfway up the side of the ceramic dish. Bake for 1 hour. Whisk mixture; cover, bake a further 30 minutes or until a golden caramel colour, adding extra boiling water to baking dish as needed to maintain water level during baking. Remove dish from water; cool. Whisk mixture until smooth. Transfer to a medium bowl; cover, refrigerate until chilled.

prep + cook time 3 hours (+ cooling) **serves** 12

nutritional count per serving 12.4g total fat (8g saturated fat); 1354kJ (323 cal); 50.5g carbohydrate; 4.8g protein; 0.5g fibre

tips Dulce de leche is a caramel spread. If you prefer, you can use ready-made dulce de leche sold in jars from delis, gourmet food stores and supermarkets. Plain honeycomb is available from some sweet stores or greengrocers. If unavailable, use two 50g (1½-ounce) Crunchie bars and cut off the chocolate. Blowtorches are available from homeware and hardware stores. Alternatively, you can place the bananas under a hot grill (broiler) to caramelise the sugar. Dulce de leche can be made a day ahead. Meringue is best made on day of serving. Store in an airtight container and assemble close to serving.

GLOSSARY

almonds

flaked paper-thin slices.

ground also called almond meal; almonds are powdered to a coarse flour-like texture.

slivered small pieces cut lengthways.

anchovies small oily fish. Anchovy fillets are preserved and packed in oil or salt in small cans or jars, and are strong in flavour. Fresh anchovies are much milder in flavour.

artichoke hearts tender centre of the globe artichoke; can be harvested from the plant after the prickly choke is removed. Cooked hearts can be bought from delicatessens or canned in brine.

baking paper also called parchment paper or baking parchment – is a silicone-coated paper that is primarily used for lining baking pans and oven trays so cakes and biscuits won't stick, making removal easy.

barley a nutritious grain used in soups and stews. Hulled barley, the least processed, is high in fibre. Pearl barley has had the husk removed then been steamed and polished so that only the "pearl" of the original grain remains, much the same as white rice.

beans

broad (fava) also called windsor and horse beans; available dried, fresh, canned and frozen. Fresh should be peeled twice (discarding both the outer long green pod and the beige-green tough inner skin); frozen beans have had their pods removed but the beige skin still needs removal.

white a generic term we use for canned or dried cannellini, haricot, navy or great northern beans belonging to the same family, *phaseolus vulgaris*.

beetroot (beets) also known as red beets; firm, round root vegetable.

brioche French in origin; a rich, yeast-leavened, cake-like bread made with butter and eggs. Available from cake or specialty bread shops.

broccolini a cross between broccoli and chinese kale; long asparagus-like stems with a long loose floret, both completely edible. Resembles broccoli but is milder and sweeter in taste.

buk choy also called bok choy, pak choi, chinese white cabbage or chinese chard; has a fresh, mild mustard taste.

burghul also called bulgar wheat; hulled steamed wheat kernels that, once dried, are crushed into various sized grains. Used in felafel, kibbeh and tabbouleh. Is not the same as cracked wheat.

butter we use salted butter unless stated otherwise; 125g is equal to 1 stick (4 ounces).

buttermilk originally the term given to the slightly sour liquid left after butter was churned from cream, today it is made from no-fat or low-fat milk to which specific bacterial cultures have been added. Despite its name, it is actually low in fat.

capers grey-green buds of a warm climate (usually Mediterranean) shrub, sold either dried and salted or pickled in a vinegar brine. Capers must be rinsed well before using.

capsicum (bell pepper) available in many colours: red, green, yellow, orange and purplish-black. Be sure to discard seeds and membranes before use.

cardamom a spice native to India and used extensively in its cuisine; sold in pod, seed or ground form. Has a distinctive aromatic and sweetly rich flavour.

celeriac (celery root) tuberous root with knobbly brown skin, white flesh and a celery-like flavour. Keep peeled celeriac in acidulated water to stop it discolouring. It can be grated and eaten raw in salads; used in soups and stews; boiled and mashed like potatoes; or sliced thinly and deep-fried as chips.

cheese

bocconcini walnut-sized, baby mozzarella, a delicate, semi-soft, white cheese traditionally made from buffalo milk. Sold fresh, it spoils rapidly so will only keep, refrigerated in brine, for 1 or 2 days.

fetta Greek in origin; a crumbly textured goat- or sheep-milk cheese having a sharp, salty taste. Ripened and stored in salted whey.

fetta, persian is a soft, creamy cheese marinated in a blend of olive oil, garlic, herbs and spices. It is available from most major supermarkets.

goat's made from goat's milk, has an earthy, strong taste. Available in soft, crumbly and firm textures, in various shapes and sizes, and sometimes rolled in ash or herbs.

haloumi a Greek Cypriot cheese with a semi-firm, spongy texture and very salty sweet flavour. Ripened and stored in salted whey; best grilled or fried, it holds its shape well on being heated. Eat while still warm as it becomes tough and rubbery on cooling.

mascarpone an Italian fresh cultured-cream product made in much the same way as yoghurt. Whiteish to creamy yellow in colour, with a buttery-rich, luscious texture. Soft, creamy and spreadable, it is used in Italian desserts and as an accompaniment to fresh fruit.

mozzarella soft, spun-curd cheese; originating in southern Italy where it was traditionally made from water-buffalo milk. Is the most popular pizza cheese because of its low melting point and elasticity when heated.

parmesan also called parmigiano; is a hard, grainy cow-milk cheese originating in Italy. Reggiano is the best variety.

ricotta a soft, sweet, moist, white cow-milk cheese with a low fat content and a slightly grainy texture. The name roughly translates as "cooked again" and refers to ricotta's manufacture from a whey that is a by-product of other cheese making.

chicken

breast fillet breast halved, skinned and boned.

marylands leg and thigh still connected in a single piece; bones and skin intact.

chickpeas (garbanzo beans) also known as hummus or channa; an irregularly round, sandy-coloured legume used extensively in Mediterranean, Indian and Hispanic cooking. Firm texture even after cooking, a floury mouth-feel and robust nutty flavour; available canned or dried (reconstitute for several hours in cold water before use).

chilli use rubber gloves when seeding and chopping fresh chillies as they can burn your skin. Removing membranes and seeds lessens the heat level.

chinese five spice a fragrant mixture of ground cinnamon, cloves, star anise, sichuan pepper and fennel seeds. Used in Chinese and other Asian cooking; available from most supermarkets or Asian food shops.

chocolate

dark (semi-sweet) also called luxury chocolate; made of a high percentage of cocoa liquor and cocoa butter, and little added sugar.

white contains no cocoa solids but derives its sweet flavour from cocoa butter. Very sensitive to heat.

cinnamon available in pieces (called sticks or quills) and ground into powder; one of the world's most common spices.

coconut

cream obtained commercially from the first pressing of the coconut flesh alone, without the addition of water; the second pressing (less rich) is sold as coconut milk. Available in cans and cartons at most supermarkets.

desiccated concentrated, dried, unsweetened and finely shredded coconut flesh.

flaked dried flaked coconut flesh.

milk not the liquid found inside the fruit (coconut water), but the diluted liquid from the second pressing of the white flesh of a mature coconut. Available in cans and cartons at most supermarkets.

cream

pouring also called pure or fresh cream. It has no additives and contains a minimum fat content of 35%.

thick (double) a dolloping cream with a minimum fat content of 45%.

thickened (heavy) a whipping cream that contains a thickener. It has a minimum fat content of 35%.

cream of tartar the acid ingredient in baking powder; added to confectionery mixtures to help prevent sugar from crystallising. Keeps frostings creamy and improves volume when beating egg whites.

crème fraîche a mature, naturally fermented cream (minimum fat content 35%) having a velvety texture and slightly tangy, nutty flavour. Crème fraîche, a French variation of sour cream, can boil without curdling and be used in sweet and savoury dishes.

cumin also known as zeera or comino; resembling caraway in size. Its spicy, almost curry-like flavour is essential to the traditional foods of Mexico, India, North Africa and the Middle East. Available dried as seeds or ground.

dukkah an Egyptian specialty spice mixture made up of roasted nuts, seeds and an array of aromatic spices.

eggplant also known as aubergine. Ranging in size from tiny to very large and in colour from pale green to deep purple. Can also be purchased char-grilled, packed in oil, in jars.

fennel also called finocchio or anise; a crunchy green vegetable slightly resembling celery that's eaten raw in salads; fried as an accompaniment; or used as an ingredient in soups, sauces and many other dishes.

flour

plain (all-purpose) unbleached wheat flour, is the best for baking: the gluten content ensures a strong dough, for a light result.

rice very fine, almost powdery, gluten-free flour; made from ground white rice. Used in baking, as a thickener, and in some Asian noodles and desserts. Another variety, made from glutinous sweet rice, is used for chinese dumplings and rice paper.

self-raising all-purpose flour with baking powder and salt added; make at home in the proportion of 1 cup flour to 2 teaspoons baking powder.

gai lan also known as chinese broccoli, gai larn, kanah, gai lum and chinese kale; appreciated more for its stems than its coarse leaves.

garam masala a blend of spices that includes cardamom, cinnamon, coriander, cloves, fennel and cumin. Black pepper and chilli can also be added for heat.

ginger

fresh also called green or root ginger; thick gnarled root of a tropical plant.

glacé fresh ginger root preserved in sugar syrup; crystallised ginger (sweetened with cane sugar) can be substituted if rinsed with warm water and dried before using.

ground also called powdered ginger; used as a flavouring in baking but cannot be substituted for fresh ginger.

harissa a Moroccan paste made from dried chillies, cumin, garlic, oil and caraway seeds. Available from Middle Eastern food shops and supermarkets.

hoisin sauce a thick, sweet and spicy Chinese barbecue sauce made from salted fermented soybeans, onions and garlic; used as a marinade or baste. Sold in supermarkets and Asian food shops.

horseradish cream is a commercially prepared creamy paste consisting of grated horseradish, vinegar, oil and sugar.

kaffir lime leaves also called bai magrood, sold fresh, dried or frozen; looks like two glossy dark green leaves joined end to end, forming a rounded hourglass shape. A strip of fresh lime peel may be substituted for each kaffir lime leaf.

kumara (orange sweet potato) Polynesian name of an orange-fleshed sweet potato often confused with yam.

lamb

cutlet small, tender rib chop; also sold french-trimmed, with all the fat and gristle at the narrow end of the bone removed.

leg cut from the hindquarter; sold boned, butterflied, rolled and tied.

shank forequarter leg; sometimes sold as drumsticks or frenched shanks if the gristle and narrow end of the bone are removed and the remaining meat trimmed.

shoulder large, tasty piece having much connective tissue so is best pot-roasted or braised. Makes the best mince.

leeks a member of the onion family, the leek resembles a green onion but is much larger and more subtle in flavour. Tender baby or pencil leeks can be eaten whole with minimal cooking but adult leeks are usually trimmed of most of the green tops then chopped and cooked.

lemon grass also called takrai, serai or serah. A tall, clumping, lemon-smelling and tasting, sharp-edged aromatic tropical grass; the white lower part of the stem is used, finely chopped. Can be found fresh, dried, powdered and frozen, in supermarkets, greengrocers and Asian food shops.

lentils (red, brown, yellow) dried pulse often identified by and named after their colour. Lentils have high food value.

maple syrup, pure distilled from the sap of sugar maple trees found only in Canada and the USA. Maple-flavoured syrup or pancake syrup is not an adequate substitute for the real thing.

muslin inexpensive, undyed, loosely woven cotton fabric called for in cooking to strain stocks and sauces.

mustard

dijon pale brown, distinctively flavoured, mild-tasting french mustard.

wholegrain also known as seeded mustard. A French-style coarse-grain mustard made from crushed mustard seeds and Dijon-style french mustard.

oil

cooking spray we use a cooking spray made from canola oil.

olive made from ripened olives. Extra virgin and virgin are the first and second press, respectively, of the olives; "light" refers to taste not fat levels.

peanut pressed from ground peanuts; most commonly used oil in Asian cooking because of its high smoke point (capacity to handle high heat without burning).

vegetable oils sourced from plant rather than animal fats.

onions

green (scallions) also called, incorrectly, shallot; an immature onion picked before the bulb has formed, has a long, bright-green stalk.

red also known as spanish, red spanish or bermuda onion; a sweet-flavoured, large, purple-red onion.

shallots also called french or golden shallots or eschalots; small and brown-skinned.

orange blossom water concentrated flavouring from orange blossoms.

pancetta an Italian unsmoked bacon; used sliced or chopped.

panko (japanese) breadcrumbs are available in two kinds: larger pieces and fine crumbs; have a lighter texture than Western-style ones. Available from Asian food stores and most supermarkets.

parsnip their nutty sweetness is especially good when steamed and dressed with a garlic and cream sauce or in a curried parsnip soup, or simply baked. Can be substituted for potatoes. Available all year but the cold develops their sweet/savoury flavour in winter.

persimmons there are two types of persimmons: an astringent one, eaten soft and a non-astringent firm variety, also known as fuji fruit.

pine nuts not a nut but a small, cream-coloured kernel from pine cones. They are best toasted before use to bring out the flavour.

polenta also known as cornmeal; a ground, flour-like cereal made of dried corn (maize). Also the name of the dish made from it.

pomegranate dark-red, leathery-skinned fruit about the size of an orange filled with hundreds of seeds, each wrapped in an edible lucent-crimson pulp with a unique tangy sweet-sour flavour.

quinoa pronounced keen-wa; is a gluten-free grain. It has a delicate, slightly nutty taste and chewy texture.

radicchio a red-leafed Italian chicory with a refreshing bitter taste that's eaten raw and grilled. Comes in varieties named after their places of origin, such as round-headed Verona or long-headed Treviso.

rhubarb a plant with long, green-red stalks; becomes sweet and edible when cooked.

roasting/toasting nuts and dried coconut can be roasted in the oven to restore their fresh flavour and release their aromatic essential oils. Spread them evenly onto an oven tray then roast in a moderate oven for about 5 minutes. Pine nuts, sesame seeds and desiccated coconut toast more evenly if stirred over low heat in a heavy-based frying pan.

silver beet (swiss chard) also called, incorrectly, spinach; has fleshy stalks and large leaves and can be prepared as for spinach.

spinach also called english spinach and incorrectly, silver beet. Baby spinach leaves are best eaten raw in salads or cooked until barely wilted.

sugar

brown a very soft, finely granulated sugar that retains molasses for its colour and flavour.

caster (superfine) finely granulated table sugar.

demerara small-grained golden-coloured crystal sugar.

icing (confectioners') also called powdered sugar; pulverised granulated sugar crushed together with a small amount of cornflour (cornstarch).

palm also called nam tan pip, jaggery, jawa or gula melaka; made from the sap of the sugar palm tree. Light brown to black in colour and usually sold in rock-hard cakes; use brown sugar instead.

white (granulated) coarse, granulated table sugar, also called crystal sugar.

sumac a purple-red, astringent ground spice; adds a tart, lemony flavour to dips and dressings. Can be found in Middle Eastern food stores.

sterilising jars it's important the jars be as clean as possible; make sure your hands, the preparation area, tea towels and cloths etc, are clean, too. The aim is to finish sterilising the jars and lids at the same time the preserve is ready to be bottled; the hot preserve should be bottled into hot, dry clean jars. Jars that aren't sterilised properly can cause deterioration of the preserves during storage. Always start with cleaned washed jars and lids, then following one of these methods:
(1) Put the jars and lids through the hottest cycle of a dishwasher without using any detergent.
(2) Lie the jars down in a boiler with the lids, cover them with cold water then cover the boiler with a lid. Bring the water to the boil over a high heat and boil the jars for 20 minutes.
(3) Stand the jars upright, without touching each other, on a wooden board on the lowest shelf in the oven. Turn the oven to the lowest possible temperature, close the oven door and leave jars to heat for 30 minutes. Remove the jars from the oven or dishwasher with a towel, or from the boiling water with tongs and rubber-gloved hands; the water will evaporate from hot wet jars quite quickly. Stand the jars upright and not touching each other on a wooden board, or a bench covered with a towel to protect and insulate the bench. Fill the jars as directed in the recipe; secure the lids tightly, holding jars firmly with a towel or an oven mitt. Leave the preserves at room temperature to cool before storing.

vanilla

bean dried, long, thin pod from a tropical golden orchid; the minuscule black seeds inside the bean impart a luscious flavour in baking and desserts.

extract obtained from vanilla beans infused in water; a non-alcoholic version of essence.

watercress one of the cress family, a large group of peppery greens used raw in salads, dips and sandwiches, or cooked in soups. Highly perishable, so it must be used as soon as possible after purchase.

yeast (dried and fresh), a raising agent used in dough making. Granular (7g sachets) and fresh compressed (20g blocks) yeast can almost always be substituted for the other.

yoghurt we use plain full-cream yoghurt in our recipes.

Greek-style plain yoghurt strained in a cloth (traditionally muslin) to remove the whey and to give it a creamy consistency.

za'atar a Middle Eastern herb and spice mixture which varies but always includes thyme, with ground sumac and, usually, toasted sesame seeds.

zucchini also called courgette; small, pale- or dark-green or yellow vegetable of the squash family. Harvested when young, its edible flowers can be stuffed and deep-fried.

CONVERSION CHART

MEASURES

One Australian metric measuring cup holds approximately 250ml; one Australian metric tablespoon holds 20ml; one Australian metric teaspoon holds 5ml. The difference between one country's measuring cups and another's is within a two- or three-teaspoon variance, and will not affect your cooking results. North America, New Zealand and the United Kingdom use a 15ml tablespoon.

All cup and spoon measurements are level. The most accurate way of measuring dry ingredients is to weigh them. When measuring liquids, use a clear glass or plastic jug with the metric markings.

The imperial measurements used in these recipes are approximate only. Measurements for cake pans are approximate only. Using same-shaped cake pans of a similar size should not affect the outcome of your baking. We measure the inside top of the cake pan to determine sizes.

We use large eggs with an average weight of 60g.

DRY MEASURES

metric	imperial
15g	½oz
30g	1oz
60g	2oz
90g	3oz
125g	4oz (¼lb)
155g	5oz
185g	6oz
220g	7oz
250g	8oz (½lb)
280g	9oz
315g	10oz
345g	11oz
375g	12oz (¾lb)
410g	13oz
440g	14oz
470g	15oz
500g	16oz (1lb)
750g	24oz (1½lb)
1kg	32oz (2lb)

LIQUID MEASURES

metric	imperial
30ml	1 fluid oz
60ml	2 fluid oz
100ml	3 fluid oz
125ml	4 fluid oz
150ml	5 fluid oz
190ml	6 fluid oz
250ml	8 fluid oz
300ml	10 fluid oz
500ml	16 fluid oz
600ml	20 fluid oz
1000ml (1 litre)	1¾ pints

LENGTH MEASURES

metric	imperial
3mm	$^1/8$in
6mm	¼in
1cm	½in
2cm	¾in
2.5cm	1in
5cm	2in
6cm	2½in
8cm	3in
10cm	4in
13cm	5in
15cm	6in
18cm	7in
20cm	8in
22cm	9in
25cm	10in
28cm	11in
30cm	12in (1ft)

OVEN TEMPERATURES

The oven temperatures in this book are for conventional ovens; if you have a fan-forced oven, decrease the temperature by 10-20 degrees.

	°C (Celsius)	°F (Fahrenheit)
Very slow	120	250
Slow	150	300
Moderately slow	160	325
Moderate	180	350
Moderately hot	200	400
Hot	220	425
Very hot	240	475

INDEX